Adalbert Rückerl

The Investigation of Nazi Crimes

The Investigation of Nazi Crimes 1945–1978

A Documentation

by

Adalbert Rückerl

Head of the Central Office
of Land Judicial Authorities
for the Investigation of National-Socialist Crimes

Translated by
Derek Rutter, Bonn

1980 Archon Books

© Adalbert Rückerl 1980

First published 1980 as an Archon Book,
an imprint of The Shoe String Press, Inc.,
Hamden, Connecticut 06514

Library of Congress Cataloging in Publication Data

Rückerl, Adalbert, 1925 –
  The investigation of Nazi crimes, 1945-1978.

  Translation of Die Strafverfolgung national-sozialistischer
Verbrechen 1945 bis 1978.
  Includes bibliographical references.
    1. War crime trials—Germany. 2. War crime trials—Europe. 3.
War crimes. I. Title. Law 341.6'9   80-20485
ISBN 0-208-01883-2

Preface

Except for those cases where limitation has been interrupted, all Nazi crimes will become statute-barred under current German law on 31 December 1979. With this in mind, it seemed a good idea to me to trace the sequence of events which have taken place since 1945 in the investigation and prosecution of Nazi crimes. The following documentation, based on the omnibus volume "Nazi Trials" of which two editions were published in 1971 and 1972, reveals something of the difficulties inherent in the prosecuting of Nazi crimes. In addition, it exposes once again the whole scale and horror of these iniquitous deeds.

I have also provided a short account of the legal fundament underlying the due processes of law to help the reader understand the workings of our criminal prosecution system. This documentation thus assumes a certain significance in finding an answer to the question we are all asking ourselves: should the legislators abolish the limitation of murder or should they leave the law as it now stands?

Unless otherwise stated, the figures quoted in the text and annexes are based on data provided by the Federal Ministry of Justice or the Central Office of the Land Judicial Authorities in Ludwigsburg. The numbers in the text refer to the notes set out at the end of the book in chapter form.

December, 1978.   *The Author and the Publisher*

Table of Contents

A. Nazi Crimes

I The first Acts of Violence against Political Opponents

No sooner had Hitler taken over the reins of government on 30 January 1933 than the National Socialists hastened to unleash a campaign of oppression and terror against their political adversaries. The first blows were struck against Communists, Socialists and trade unionists; but the operation soon expanded to cover the supporters of the democratic middle-class parties, too.

On 28th February 1933, the very next day after the fire at the Reichstag building, President von Hindenburg signed the "Emergency Decree for the Protection of the Nation and the State"[1] — thus setting aside for an unlimited period of time the fundamental rights embodied in the Constitution. The police were authorized to seize political opponents, free from any judicial supervision, and to take them into "protective custody" for an unlimited period of time. This protective custody was not deemed to be a means of punishing criminal acts, but a "preventive" police measure designed to eliminate the "dangers emanating from enemies of the State"[2]. The Nazis exploited this device to bring about the arbitrary arrest of a great many people holding different political views. The SA[3], a quasi-militia founded by the National Socialist Party[4] and often enlisted as an auxiliary police force in the following weeks and months, was given more or less a free hand in setting up concentration camps all over Germany[5]. The most important establishments of this kind, now referred to by students of modern history as "early concentration camps", stood in Ahrensbök (Holstein), Ankenbuch (Baden), Bad Sulza (Thuringia), Benninghausen (Westphalia), Berlin-Columbia-Haus, Börgermoor (Emsland), Brandenburg, Brauweiler (near Cologne), Breitenau (near Cassel), Bremen-Findorf, Bremerhaven, Breslau-Dürrgoy, Colditz (Saxony)), Dachau (near Munich), Dresden, Esterwegen (Emsland), Gollnov (near Stettin), Hainichen (Saxony), Hammerstein (Pomerania), **Hamburg-Fuhlsbüttel, Heuberg (Wurttemberg)**, Hohnstein (Saxony), Kemna (near Wuppertal), Kislau (Baden), Moringen (near Göttingen), Oranienburg (near Berlin), Osthofen (near Worms), Resslau (near Dessau), Sachsenburg (Saxony), Sonnenburg (Mark Brandenburg), Stettin-Bredow, Ulm-Kuhberg, Werden (Ruhr District), Wittmoor (near Hamburg), Zwickau (Saxony) and Lichtenburg (near Torgau).

The illegal camps known as "wilde Konzentrationslager" became notorious for their atrocities. These places were set up on an unsupervised and temporary basis by a number of SA units, who usually chose empty factories or houses for the purpose.

A circular issued by the Reich Minister of the Interior on 11 September 1933 shows that 26,789 people were in protective custody in Germany as of 31 July 1933[6]. Even though there is nothing to show that Nazi leaders were already contemplating the physical extermination of their political opponents when they set up these camps and connived at the cruelties perpetrated in them, the fact remains that these early and unsanctioned camps resulted in the death of numerous inmates.

II The Röhm Putsch

The rivalry felt between the SA as the party militia and the regular army led in the Spring of 1934 to strained relations between Hitler and the SA's Chief of Staff, Ernst Röhm. Acting on the pretence that Röhm was planning a revolt, Hitler with the support of Goering and Heinrich

Himmler (Head of the SS) ordered the arrest on 30 June 1934 of the SA Chief and numerous other senior SA leaders and had them shot the same day or following morning[7]. The opportunity was also taken to get rid of a number of political rivals such as the former Reich Chancellor, General von Schleicher and his wife, General von Bredow (the Head of "Catholic Action"), Ministerial-Director Klausener and the former Bavarian Minister President, Herr von Kahr[8].

With a view to providing a legal basis for these murders, Hitler's Government — able since the "Enabling Act" came into force on 24 March 1933[9] to do as it pleased without any consideration for democratic supervisory bodies — passed a law only three days later, i.e. on 3 July 1934[10], declaring the deeds to have been legal executive measures carried out in a national emergency.

III Concentration Camps

All the "wilde Konzentrationslager" and most of the "early camps" were disbanded during the Summer of 1933 and replaced in the course of time by a number of large camps under the control of the "Inspektion der Konzentrationslager" and, from 1942, the SS Economic Administrative Office[11,12]. By the beginning of the War, a total of 21,400 prisoners were being detained in standardized camps comprising Dachau, Sachsenhausen, Buchenwald, Mauthausen, Flossenbürg and Ravensbrück. With few exceptions, all the prisoners were German nationals.

In the course of the next two years, the following camps were added to the list: Auschwitz (near Kattowitz), Bergen-Belsen (near Uelzen), Gross-Rosen (Silesia), Herzogenbusch (Holland), Kauen (Lithuania), Klooga (Estonia), Lublin-Maidanek ("Generalgouvernement"), Mittelbau Dora (near Nordhausen in the Harz Mountains), Natzweiler (Alsace), Neuengamme (near Hamburg), Niederhagen-Wewelsburg (near Paderborn), Plaszov ("Generalgouvernement"), Riga-Kaiserwald (Latria), Stutthof (Danzig-West Prussia), Vaivara (Estonia) and the special camp Hinzert in the Hunsrück Mountains.

As industry began to require more and more prisoners as a labour force, hundreds of subsidiary and branch camps began to spring up within the immediate or more distant vicinity of the main camps: they were, however, administered by the latter and therefore subject to the control of the SS Economic Administrative Office[13]. At the beginning of 1945, the concentration and subsidiary camps together housed over 600,000 prisoners of various nationalities.

The various categories of prisoner — political detainees, homosexuals, Jehovah's Witnesses, gipsies, delinquents and professional criminals — wore coloured triangles to distinguish which group they belonged to. On the grounds or pretence that they belonged to one of these groups, the Jews were also committed to the concentration camps where they had to wear an additional yellow distinguishing mark.

As a rule, the fate of concentration camp inmates was determined by two official agencies marked by differing objectives. The Reich Security Office, which held the exclusive right to order someone's detention in a camp, was primarily interested in the elimination (including physical liquidation) of prisoners regarded as opponents. On the other hand, the SS Economic Administrative Office[14] was interested in the brutal exploitation of prisoners as a source of labour. This contrast became particularly manifest in the two concentration camps of Auschwitz and Lublin-Maidanek, simultaneously set up as extermination centres. The Reich Security Office wanted all Jews sent to the camps to be killed whereas the SS Economic Administrative Office insisted on singling out the able-bodied men and women.

14

Life in the concentration camps was governed by arbitrary acts and chicanery. Housed in inhuman conditions in overcrowded huts and fed on the scantiest possible rations, the prisoners were brutally maltreated, driven to suicide or tortured to death in the most atrocious manner by SS camp guards supported by obsequious camp police chosen from among the prisoners. Sick inmates were often given an injection to kill them off. On the instructions of the Head of the SS or the Reich Security Office, the concentration camps regularly became the scene of individual executions and occasionally mass shootings (especially of Russian prisoners of war). Large numbers of inmates were used in medical experiments (for example for hypothermia, sterilization and malaria) resulting in their deaths. Besides the large extermination facilities in Auschwitz and Lublin-Maidanek, smaller gas chambers had been installed at some of the other concentration camps such as Mauthausen, Ravensbruck and Natzweiler to kill prisoners with poison gas[15].

When the concentration camps had to be cleared during the final months and weeks of the War because of advancing Allied troops, the evacuation of prisoners to areas not directly threatened by invasion took place in a series of long exhausting marches. Many of the prisoners dropped dead from sheer exhaustion whilst thousands were shot by the accompanying SS guards if they proved unable to continue the forced march.

IV The "Kristallnacht"[16]

After the Nazi seizure of governmental power, the Jews (no longer "national comrades" pursuant to the Nazi Party Programme and thus not German citizens, either) became the target for a welter of slander, oppression, deprivation of rights, physical intimidation and persecution.

15

The restrictions placed upon them by statute or decree covered all aspects of life such as educational amenities, vocational opportunities, private accommodation, property and freedom of movement[17]. Large numbers of Jews were flung into the concentration camps soon after the Nazi takeover and subjected to the special torments of SS guards.

The opportunity for an organized pogrom finally came after the murder of a German diplomat, Herr von Rath, at the German Embassy in Paris by a seventeen-year-old Jewish emigrant called Hershel Grünspan on 7th November 1938. In an upsurge of national fury dubbed by Nazi propagandists as "spontaneous", the night between 9 and 10 November 1938 witnessed the demolition and burning down of synagogues, the looting of Jewish shops and homes, and the arrest, maltreatment or killing of numerous Jews. We now know from preserved documents that this "spontaneous, national fury" was an organized and centrally directed operation. According to a report forwarded by Heydrich to Göring, a total of 20,000 Jews were put under arrest, 36 severely wounded and 36 killed: 101 synagogues were set on fire and another 76 laid waste[18].

V "Euthanasia"

The outbreak of war in September 1939 also saw the beginning of a programme designed to dispose of "non-useful life", i.e. the killing of all permanently disabled mental patients. Under the control of the "Führer's Chancellery", this task devolved upon an organization operated under a variety of false designations such as the Charitable Patients Transport Society or "T 4" — named after its main office at Tiergartenstraße No. 4 in Berlin. Doctors of seemingly reliable Nazi convictions were grouped together in commissions set up to select patients for killing after summary proceedings. Although some of the killings took place in the lunatic asylums and sanatoria by doctors administering lethal injections to the patients, most of those selected for extermination went to Grafeneck in Wurttemberg, Hadamar near Limburg, Brandenburg/Havel, Bernburg in Saxony-Anhalt, Hartheim near Linz and Sonnestein near Pirna where they were put to death in gas chambers into which carbon dioxide was injected.

Under the impact of the rising tide of indignation among the population who had soon become aware of what was going on despite the efforts made to keep the operation secret and above all the courageous protests lodged by high-ranking church dignitaries, these measures finally came to an end in 1941. But the prisoner euthansia programme, i.e. the killing of concentration camp inmates unable to work and the children's euthanasia programme carried out by doctors administering lethal medicaments and injections in the special pediatric wards of the mental institutions, were both continued for a long period of time.

VI The Operational Groups in Poland and the Self-Protection Units of Ethnic Germans

A short time after the outbreak of the War, six "operational groups of Security Police and Security Service men, each comprising several units, moved behind the advancing frontline troops into occupied territory. Their mission was described to the population in general and the German army in particular as "combating all anti-Reich and anti-German elements in hostile territory behind the fighting troops". But as a secret memo written by Security Police Chief Reinhard Heydrich on 2 July 1940 reveals, the operational groups had orders to liquidate Polish leaders and the implementation of these orders resulted in the death of thousands of members of the Polish intelligentsia. The operational groups were supported by units

17

of the ethnic Self-Protection Organization, a militia consisting of local men of German extraction under the command of SS leaders from Germany. The district of the "Self-Protection Leader for Danzig-West Prussia" was the scene of many arbitrary shootings during the first weeks of the War. Although these murders by the Self-Protection units were primarily directed against members of the Polish intelligentsia or Jews, they also originated in the frequently egoistic motives of individual leaders and members of this militia.

The military commands of the Wehrmacht had no knowledge of the murderous instructions issued to these "operational groups". Like the bulk of ethnic Germans in the occupied territories, they rejected the acts of violence committed against Poles and Jews. The large number of protests sent at the time to Hitler and Goering demonstrate the prevailing view that these attacks were malpractices perpetrated by local agencies and not sanctioned by the supreme authorities. Conservative estimates put the total number of victims, almost all Poles and Jews, in the "Intelligenz-Aktion" at 60-80,000 persons. The operation came to a halt in 1940 when foreign newspapers began to report it. After the start of the attack on France in May 1940, the assumption was that world public opinion would now turn its attention to Western Europe and the extermination campaign against Polish leaders continued for several months in the Generalgouvernement under the code name AB-Aktion (allgemeine Befriedungsaktion i.e. general pacification operation).

VII The Security Police and Security Service Operational Groups in the Russian Campaign

Similar to the situation in Autumn 1939 at the beginning of the Polish campaign, four operational groups (A, B, C and D) under the command of the Chief of Security Police and the Security Service — subdivided into four or five special units — were set up in May 1941 for the attack on Russia. This force comprised members of the Security Police (Gestapo and Criminal Police) and the Security Service, later to be reinforced by a battalion of police reserves and a battalion of Waffen SS. In line with agreements already concluded in March 1941 between the Supreme Command of the armed forces and the Security Police, the operational groups and units were not only to discharge specific police duties during the campaign against Russia but also to carry out "executive measures" against the civilian population pursuant to instructions issued by the Head of the SS or the Reich Security Office. The operational groups were only accountable to the Head of the SS and not to the army authorities for their activities. A short time after the launching of the invasion of Russia in June 1941, the operational groups and units received orders to "solve the Jewish problem" — as a number of reports put it — in their allotted area of operations: all Jews not needed as workers were to be liquidated. Other categories of persons such as political commissars, gipsies and lunatics were also to be killed. The executions usually took place in the form of mass shootings though, in some cases, the gas vans were used.

Each operational group submitted regular accounts to the Reich Security Office on its "achievements". The Office then issued a general "Progress Report for the USSR". According to the Progress Report, the total number of victims amounted to 560,000 by April 1942 with group A accounting for 250,000, B for 70,000, C for 150,000 and D for 90,000.

When civilian authorities were set up in the occupied Eastern territories, the mobile operational groups and units became static agencies.

They continued their campaign of exterminating Jews and gipsies and began by sending all Jews to the ghettos organized in all of the big cities. The inhabitants of the ghettos were then gradually killed off during execution operations disguised as "resettlement programmes". Quite often, these resettlement schemes cost thousands their lives as for example in the ghetto at Pinsk, when about 10,000 people were murdered on the first of a two-day operation.

VIII Nazi Crimes during the Fight against Partisans

At the beginning, quite a lot of the Soviet civilian population did not adopt a hostile attitude towards German soldiers. However, the brutal measures taken by the units of security and administrative police against certain categories of civilians contrary to the interests and wishes of most military commanders succeeded in swelling the ranks of the isolated and fairly weak groups of partisans and thus in making them a serious threat to all troops behind the lines.

The police units called in to deal with the partisans frequently reacted to the partisans' internationally illegal combat methods with merciless rigour and cruelty on a scale that was a flagrant contravention of international law. Villages and farms near places where partisans had been sighted were destroyed and the inhabitants (including women and children) put to death. A report from the Head of the SS to Hitler dated 29 December 1942 noted that in South Russia, the Ukraine and the district of Bialystok alone a total of 150 villages and 1,978 large farms had been burnt down or razed to the ground.

As the operational commands and progress reports issued by police agencies and units indicate, the original order still applied that, apart from fighting partisans, they had to kill all Jews encountered during operations "independent of the reprisals".

The progress reports contained separate entries for executed Jews, partisans killed during fighting and suspected partisan sympathisers shot after the military action. In those cases where the victims were classified, the number of women and children regularly exceeded that of the men. Jews often accounted for as much as 80 to 90% of the total number of victims[19].

IX The "Final Solution of the Jewish Question"

Up to Autumn 1941, the large-scale organized measures to bring about the physical destruction of the Jews took place almost exclusively in Polish and Soviet territories occupied by the German armed forces. We hear of few cases at that time of "resettlement transports" involving the movement of Jews from Germany to Eastern areas for extermination purposes.

On 20 January 1942, the Chief of the Security Police and Security Service Reinhard Heydrich submitted to the senior representatives of various governmental, SS and police departments assembled at the "Wannsee Conference" in Berlin a plan for the "final solution of the Jewish question in Europe" and designed in the last analysis to bring about the physical annihilation of all European Jews. Under this comprehensive plan, the Jews concentrated in the ghettos in the Generalgouvernement and the Wartheland were sent to the extermination camps to be killed by means of motor exhaust fumes or the poison gas cyclon B. The vacant areas of the ghettos were then used to house Jews from other occupied territories or from Germany before these in turn met their death in the extermination camps.

The camps at Chelmno, Belzec, Sobibor and Treblinka, where Jews were killed by motor exhaust fumes, served exclusively for extermination purposes. On the other hand, the big camps at Auschwitz and Lublin-Maidanek, which used poisonous cyclon B for mass killings, served

21

simultaneously as an extermination and a concentration camp. During the trials of the camp personnel, the courts ascertained pursuant to the available evidence that the minimum number of people killed by gas amounted to 152,000 in Chelmno, 390,000 in Belzec, 150,000 in Sobibor and 700,000 in Treblinka. On each occasion, the courts stressed that these were the indisputable minimum figures on which their sentences had been based: the number of victims as computed by German and foreign historians stands much higher.

In effect, the investigation and research carried out to date suggest a figure of well over a million people killed in the gas chambers of Auschwitz. By the same token, the estimates for Lublin-Maidanek are far in excess of 200,000[20].

When Jews were being rounded up in the ghettos of the Generalgouvernement for transportation to the extermination camps, sick persons and others unfit for travel were as a rule simply shot on the spot. In cases where the removal of Jews to extermination camps from ghettos not located along the railway routes seemed to present too many transport difficulties, a series of "local resettlements" took place. The Jews were shot in secluded places near their homes and hurriedly buried in previously dug mass graves. In order to make sure that — if at all possible — no Jews escaped extermination, local police agencies had orders to shoot out of hand any Jew encountered without a permit outside of the ghetto.

X Crimes committed against Prisoners of War

Large numbers of prisoners of war were shot on the strength of various commands and decrees issued by the supreme military authorities.

The "Commissar Order" issued by the High Command of the German armed forces decreed the killing of Soviet commissars immediately after capture. The "Commando

Order", also issued by the High Command stipulated the killing of commando troops operating behind German lines. The "Bullet Decree" issued by the Army's Supreme Command concerned the killing of escaped prisoners of war who had been recaptured. Whereas the execution of these three orders only produced a small number of victims, "operational orders Nos. 8, 9 and 14 of the Chief of Security Police and the Security Service" led to the searching by Security Policy and Security Service detachments of army prison camps where they found and subsequently shot thousands of Soviet prisoners of war who were either Jews or suspected Communist officials.

XI Other Criminal Acts

Many of the Polish and Russian slave workers carried off to Germany were killed without any trial upon instructions from the Reich Security Office because of some insignificant infringement of the strict rules of conduct. The last months of the War were also marked by the sporadic murdering of foreign workers to prevent their liberation by advancing Allied troops. In addition, many people met their death during the last weeks of the War pursuant to a court-martial sentence or to SS or Nazi Party instructions because they had tried to prevent further bloodshed in their local town upon the approach of the Allies by such acts as hoisting a white flag.

In addition, thousands of civilians were killed in countries occupied during the War by the German army without these murders being classifiable under the series of crimes listed above in chapters I to X. Most of the deeds were perpetrated by members of the Security Police and some by members of other organizations: the purpose of these operations was to consolidate the reign of terror.

Mention should also be made of the individual crimes committed for personal motives and not prosecuted because of the political situation existing at the time.

B. Prosecution by Allied and Foreign Courts

I The Trials at the International Military Tribunal in Nuremberg

Even when the War was still on, the Allies had agreed to take into their own hands the elimination of National Socialism and the punishment of its leaders and officials once the hostilities ended.

Under the terms of the Moscow Declaration announced on 1 November 1943 by the three major allied powers (the USA, Great Britain and the Soviet Union) engaged in the struggle against Germany, anyone participating in Nazi and war crimes was to be tried by the courts of those states on whose territory the crimes had been committed[1].

Explicitly excluded from this were the major war criminals[2], whose deeds could not be limited to any defined geographical area: they would be punished in accordance with a joint decision to be taken by the Governments of the Allied powers. This joint decision was adopted on 8 August 1945 in the "Agreement on the Punishment of the Major War Criminals of the European Axis" signed by 23 states. The statute appended to this Agreement decreed the setting up of an international court of law by Great Britain, the USA, France and the Soviet Union to pronounce judgment on the deeds committed by that category of persons.

Of the leading Nazi figures, 24 had to face trial before the International Military Tribunal in Nuremberg on charges relating to the crimes listed in the above-mentioned statute: preparations for a war of aggression (1), crimes against peace (2), war crimes (3) or crimes against humanity (4). One of the accused, Dr. Robert Ley (Head of

Reich Organization) committed suicide before the hearings opened. In the case of the industrialist Gustav Krupp von Bohlen und Halbach, the court directed separate proceedings for the accused because of his unfitness for trial. After trials lasting over 10 months, the following persons out of the 22 remaining accused heard the court's sentences on 1 October 1946.

— Reich Marshal Hermann Göring, the death sentence (on charges 1, 2, 3 and 4)
— Hitler's deputy Rudolf Hess, imprisonment for life (1 and 2)
— Foreign Minister Joachim von Ribbentrop, the death sentence (1, 2, 3 and 4)
— Field Marshal Wilhelm Keitel, Chief of the High Command of the Armed Forces, the death sentence (1, 2, 3 and 4)
— SS-Obergruppenführer Ernst Kaltenbrunner, Chief of the Reich Security Office, the death sentence (3 and 4)
— Minister for the occupied Eastern territories, Alfred Rosenberg, the death sentence (1, 2, 3 and 4)
— the Generalgouverneur for Poland, Hans Frank, the death sentence (3 and 4)
— the Gauleiter of Franconia and publisher of the virulently anti-Jewish paper "Der Stürmer", Julius Streicher, the death sentence (4)
— Minister for Economic Affairs, Walter Funk, imprisonment for life (2, 3 and 4)
— Admiral Karl Dönitz, Supreme Commander of the German Navy, a term of 10 years imprisonment (2 and 3)
— Admiral Ernst Raeder, Dönitz's predecessor in office as Supreme Commander of the German Navy, imprisonment for life (1, 2 and 3)

- Reich Youth Leader and Gauleiter of Vienna, Baldur von Schirach, 20 years imprisonment (4)
- the Gauleiter of Thuringia and Reich Commissioner for Labour, Fritz Sauckel, the death sentence (3, 4)
- Minister of the Interior Wilhelm Frick, the death sentence (2, 3, 4)
- Minister of Armaments Albert Speer, 20 years imprisonment
- Colonel-General Alfred Jodl, Chief of Military Operations Staff, the death sentence (1, 2, 3, 4)
- Minister for the Netherlands, Artur Seyß-Inquart, the death sentence (2, 3, 4)
- Minister of Foreign Affairs and Reich Protector for Bohemia and Moravia, Constantin von Neurath, 15 years imprisonment (1, 2, 3, 4)
- Reichsleiter and Chief of the Party Chancellery, Martin Bormann, the death sentence — in absentia (3, 4) [2a]

Three men were acquitted against the vote of the Soviet judge: Hans Fritsche (Departmental Head at the Ministry of Propaganda); Franz von Papen (Vice-Chancellor and later German ambassador to Austria and Turkey); and Hjalmar Schacht (President of the Reich Bank and Minister of Economic Affairs).

II Trials by Allied Courts [3]

The original Allied plan to hold further trials before the International Military Tribunal of persons holding senior positions in Germany during the Nazi régime was not carried out. Pursuant to Control Council Law No. 10 dated 20 December 1945, which set out the crimes listed in the statute to the London Agreement [4], judgment was to be pronounced in the various zones of occupation by the courts of the competent occupying power.

1. Trials by American Military Tribunals

Twelve major trials were held by the American Military Tribunal in Nuremberg up to the middle of 1949:

a) The "doctors' case" involving 23 persons accused of taking part in the "euthanasia programme", carrying out cruel and dangerous experiments on human beings and killing concentration-camp inmates for the purpose of obtaining a set of skeletons;

b) The trial of Field Marshal Milch on a charge of taking part in the War Armaments Programme;

c) The "lawyers' case" involving 16 leading jurists and presiding judges at special courts;

d) The trial of 18 members of the SS Economic Administrative Office, which was responsible for running the concentration camps;

e) The trial of the industrialist Friedrich Flick and 5 of his staff on a charge of exploiting slave labour and plundering foreign property;

f) The trial of 23 senior executives of "IG-Farben" on charges of conspiring to unleash a war of aggression, indulging in economic plundering and exploiting the labour of prisoners of war, deportees and concentration-camp inmates (particularly in Auschwitz);

g) The "hostages case" or "case of the Balkan generals" against 12 senior officers accused of the unlawful shooting of hostages in the Balkans;

h) The "Ru SHA Process" involving 14 senior members from the SS Office for Reich and Resettlement Matters, the Office of the "Reich Commissar for strengthening the German Race", the Lebensborn (Spring of Life) Organization etc on charges of taking part in the annihilation of Poles and Jews and deporting "racially suitable" children from the occupied territories to Germany;

i) The "Operational Groups Case" involving 24 heads of operational groups and units of the Security Police and Security Service because of their participation in murders committed in the occupied Eastern territories;

j) The trial of Alfred Krupp von Bohlen und Halbach and 11 senior executives of his firm on a charge of plundering foreign property and exploiting slave labour;

k) The "Wilhelmstraße Case" involving 21 ministers, state secretaries, Gauleiters, senior SS officials and other prominent figures of the Nazi period accused of war crimes and crimes against humanity committed in their sphere of activity;

l) The "OKW Case" involving 14 of the most senior officers in the German armed forces on charges of committing war crimes and crimes against humanity.

Of the 184 accused in the above-mentioned twelve proceedings, 7 persons were not tried because of their illness or death whilst 35 were acquitted; 98 were sentenced to terms of imprisonment ranging from 18 months to 20 years, 20 to life sentences, and 24 to death. Of these death sentences imposed in the doctors' case (7), the trial of members of the SS Economic Administrative Office (3) and the operational groups case (14), 12 were actually carried out [5].

Among the other trials conducted by American military tribunals, special mention may be made of those against the concentration-camp guards at Dachau, Buchenwald, Mauthausen, Mittelbau-Dora and Flossenbürg. Of the 1,021 accused in these trials, 885 were convicted and 136 acquitted. As far as the judicial authorities in the Federal Republic of Germany have been able to ascertain, American military tribunals instituted proceedings against 1,941 persons of whom 1,517 were sentenced (324 to death, 247 to life imprisonment and 946 to varying terms of imprisonment)[6]. 367 of the accused were acquitted whilst in 57 cases the prosecutor withdrew the charges.

2. Trials by British Military Tribunals

British military tribunals initiated criminal proceedings against German nationals not only in the British Zone of Occupation in Germany, but also abroad (e.g. Italy and the Netherlands). In addition to the trial of Field Marshal Kesselring in Venice and that of Colonel-General von Falkenhorst and Field Marshal von Manstein in Hamburg, special mention should be made of the legal proceedings taken against the concentration-camp guards at Auschwitz, Bergen-Belsen and Natzweiler.

Of the total number of 1,085 accused tried by British military tribunals, 240 were given the death sentence. Where the tribunals inflicted terms of imprisonment, these were later mostly reduced as an act of clemency. The last Germans to serve a term of imprisonment by virtue of sentences delivered by British military tribunals were finally released in 1957.

3. Trials by French Military Tribunals

The bulk of the criminal proceedings instituted by French Occupation courts in Germany against Germans concerned the concentration-camp guards at "Neue Bremme" (near Saarbrücken) and various subsidiary camps of the concentration camp at Natzweiler in Baden-Wurttemberg. The total number of persons brought to trial before military tribunals in the French Zone of Occupation in Germany is not known: however, these courts convicted 2,107 persons (including 104 sentenced to death)[7].

In addition, military tribunals in France and French North Africa handed down sentences against at least 1,918 German nationals. To these must be added the 956 sentences delivered in absentia and ascertained by the Central Office for the Investigation of National-Socialist Crimes in Ludwigsburg on the strength of French lists.

4. *Trials by Soviet Courts*

No reliable data are available on the volume of legal proceedings instituted by Soviet courts against German nationals. It may, however, be safely assumed that the number of those convicted was many times more than the aggregate number of persons sentenced by all the tribunals of the Western occupying powers together. The following extract comes from the report forwarded by the Federal Minister of Justice to the Bundestag President on 26 February 1965 [8].

> "The occupation of Eastern and Central Germany ushered in a virtually indiscriminate spate of arrest and imprisonment of all Germans considered by the Soviets to be dangerous. Tens of thousands were sent to penitentiaries, prisons and concentration camps including for example Buchenwald, Sachsenhausen, Neubrandenburg, Mühlberg and Bautzen. Starvation and in some cases torture were used there to extract "confessions" as the basis for trials by Soviet military tribunals, i.e. if the prisoners had not already died as a result of their privations, illnesses and maltreatment.
>
> . . .
>
> Even ordinary German soldiers who had been taken prisoner appeared in their thousands before military tribunals, which usually sentenced them to uniform terms of 25 years imprisonment or in many cases to death after summary proceedings often built up on extorted confessions or simply the accused's membership of a certain military unit. One combat-engineer, for instance, received a sentence because he had used "publicly owned" timber to construct a bridge, whilst a stretcher-bearer got his for looking after soldiers wounded in the fight against the partisans. Those convicted did, however, include people who had perpetrated serious crimes such as the former concentration-camp overseers Hempel, Höhn, Schubert and Sorge or the concentration-camp physician Dr. Baumkötter, who were all later retried in the Federal Republic. Frequently, those convicted were deported to the Soviet Union to work in labour camps. There is no means of ascertaining their precise

number: according to Soviet statements, there were still 13,532 prisoners serving tribunal sentences in Russian camps as of May 1950.

Pursuant to a letter sent by General Zhukov to Ulbricht on 14 January 1950, 10,513 persons sentenced by Soviet military tribunals were surrendered to the authorities of the Soviet Zone of Occupation "for the completion of their sentence".

5. Trials by other Foreign Courts

Similarly, there are no official statistics on the criminal proceedings conducted by courts in other foreign states against Germans.

According to information received by the Central Office, the following number of accused persons were convicted in the given country:

Belgium	75 (10 death sentences),
Denmark	80 (4 death sentences),
Luxemburg	68 (15 death sentences),
Netherlands	204 (19 death sentences),
Norway	80 (16 death sentences).

Pursuant to a Press account, the Polish Minister of Justice stated at a Plenary Session of the Main Polish Commission for the Investigation of Nazi Crimes in the middle of 1978 that a total of 5,358 German nationals were sentenced during the period 1944 to 1977 for their involvement in Nazi crimes [10].

We have no knowledge of the presumably substantial number of Germans sentenced in Yugoslavia [11].

Nor are reliable data available on the number of Germans sentenced by Czech courts for war crimes and Nazi crimes.

As regards Israel, the Head of Department IV B 4 (the Jewish Dept.) at the Reich Security Office — SS Obersturmbannführer Adolf Eichmann — was tried by the district court of Jerusalem and sentenced to death. After confirmation of the verdict by the Supreme Court of the State of Israel and the refusal by the Israeli State President to grant a pardon, Eichmann was put to death on 31 May 1962.

C. The Prosecution of Nazi Crimes by German Legal Authorities in the Federal Republic of Germany from 1945 to the Present Time

If we are to present a correct assessment of the findings of legal proceedings[1] instituted against former National Socialists in the Federal Republic of Germany since the end of the War, we have to take a closer look at the historic train of events involved in the prosecuting of Nazi crimes. The investigation and prosecution of crimes committed during the Nazi reign of terror from 1933 to 1945 has been characterized by a series of different phases since the end of the War. To an outside observer, these phases may seem to have merged by imperceptible degrees but on the other hand to remain clearly demarcated.

I 1945—1950

Following the collapse of National-Socialist rule, a start was made in Germany in the summer of 1945 on re-establishing judicial administration. To begin with, the measures taken were of a tentative nature due to the complex internal and legal situation. The position became clearer after 30 November 1945 when Allied Control Council Law No. 4 on the "Reorganization of the German Judicial System" of 30 October 1945 entered into force[2]. The relevant provisions of Article III of this Law state that the "jurisdiction of German courts shall extend to all cases both civil and criminal with **the following exceptions**":

a) . . .

b) "Criminal offences committed by Nazis or any other persons against citizens of Allied nations and their property, as well as attempts directed towards the re-establishment of the Nazi régime, and the activity of the Nazi organizations".

This provision was soon replaced by Control Council Law No. 10 of 10 December 1945 on the "Punishment of Persons guilty of War Crimes, Crimes against Peace and against Humanity"[3].

Pursuant to Article II of this law, all of the following acts are deemed to constitute crimes:

"**War Crimes.** Atrocities or offences against persons or property constituting violations of the laws or customs of war, including but not limited to murder, ill-treatment or deportation of slave labour or for any other purpose, of civilian population from occupied territory, murder or ill-treatment of prisoners of war or persons on the seas, killing of hostages, plunder of public or private property, wanton destruction of cities, towns or villages or devastation not justified by military necessity.

Crimes against Humanity. Atrocities and offences, including but not limited to murder, extermination, enslavement, deportation, imprisonment, torture, rape or other inhumane acts committed against any civilian population, or persecutions on political, racial or religious grounds whether or not in violation of the domestic laws of the country where perpetrated".

The punishment provided for under Article II, fig 3 consists of the following:

a) Death.
b) Imprisonment for life or a term of years with or without hard labour.
c) Fine and imprisonment with or without hard labour in lieu thereof.
d) Fortfeiture of property wrongfully acquired.
f) Deprivation of some or all civil rights.

Article II, fig 4 states the following:

"The fact that any person acted pursuant to the order of his Government or of a superior does not free him from his responsibility for a crime, but may be considered in mitigation".

As regards the possible jurisdiction of German courts, Article III, fig 1 d states that each occupying authority, within its Zone of Occupation,

"shall have the right to cause all persons so arrested ... to be brought to trial before an appropriate tribunal. Such tribunal may in the case of crimes **committed by persons of German citizenship or nationality against other persons of German citizenship or nationality, or stateless persons,** be a German court, if authorized by the occupying authorities".

This authorization of competence, which merely comprised a prosecution of the crimes committed by Germans against Germans or stateless persons, was issued in the following period on a universal basis in the British and French Zones of Occupation and in the American Zone of Occupation on an ad hoc basis. In their punishment of Nazi crimes, the German courts had to base their findings on the provisions of Control Council Law No. 10. The provisions of German penal law could only be applied to such crimes as were not covered by the cases set out in Control Council Law No. 10. German courts were thus barred from prosecuting crimes committed against persons from the Allied nations, i.e. most of the Nazi crimes committed between 1939 and 1945.

Apart from the restrictions placed on German jurisdiction by virtue of Allied law, the investigation and punishment of Nazi crimes by German prosecuting authorities was rendered more difficult in the years after the War due to a number of circumstances.

In the past, crimes of that nature and on that scale had been unknown. The legal administrative bodies were hampered by a chronic shortage of personnel. Moreover, only a relatively small number of investigators could be used for these activities and, then again, even they lacked the requisite detailed knowledge of the background and contemporary events. The existing police force was not yet large enough to conduct thorough supra-regional investigations.

In many instances, records and registry entries had been lost during the War. By the same token, the division of Germany into four Zones of Occupation often rendered it difficult to maintain supra-regional communications. Finally, there was sometimes a lack of coordination in the investigatory activities carried out by the various public prosecutors' offices.

When the public prosecutors learnt — usually through information furnished to the police — of crimes committed during the National Socialist régime within their local area of jurisdiction, they instituted preliminary proceedings, i.e. if the valid statutory provisions or special authorization issued by the occupation authorities permitted German legal authorities to undertake criminal prosecution. At the beginning, these proceedings mostly concerned criminal acts committed in concentration camps or in conjunction with the "Röhm putsch", the "Kristallnacht" or the killing of mentally deranged persons under the euthanasia programme. In addition, the courts dealt with numerous criminal acts now designated as "crimes committed during the end phase". These were notably the execution of persons unwilling to obey the usually pointless rallying commands issued by Nazi Party organizations. Many of the executions were carried out quite arbitrarily or pursuant to court-martial findings during the final weeks of the War.

The atrocities which first became known in detail during the trials at the International Military Tribunal in Nuremberg had produced a feeling of genuine shock and profound dismay among the people of Germany. Nevertheless, many of them adopted an indifferent, reserved or even critical attitude towards the efforts of Allied and German prosecuting authorities to punish these crimes. There were a number of factors to account for this.

The most obvious reason — though probably also the gravest one in terms of its impact — consisted in the condition of Germany, devastated by bombing and economically ruined, and the fact that anyone who had survived the war more or less intact sought above all to find food and accommodation for himself and his family. At that time, many people wished to have nothing more to do with "political affairs" — and that was how they often viewed the committal for trial of Nazi officials.

The reason why they regarded the murder of millions of Jews, political opponents and insane persons as a political act rather than a primarily criminal one may be found in the reporting of the trials mounted by the International Military Tribunal in Nuremberg and its enormous impact on public opinion. The trials were characterized by an intermingling of military, political and purely criminal events in a manner which rendered it virtually impossible for an unprejudiced observer to obtain the facts needed to unravel the tangle of evidence.

There was another point. To the average citizen's way of thinking, war crimes (i.e. the legal infringements perpetrated in direct connection with military action such as had always occurred in the past between belligerent powers) occupied a lower rung on the scale of misdeeds and certainly well below criminal acts. The extension of the term "war crimes" to political events in addition to purely criminal ones, such as occasionally occurred in the formal linguistic usage of Allied courts but in any case without exception in popular speech, produced a downgrading of the trials in public opinion.

Even before the commencement of the trials at the International Military Tribunal in Nuremberg, there was talk of "victors' justice", i.e. the abuse of some aspects of judicial proceedings to wreak arbitrary revenge. The emergence at a later date of the fact that confessions had been obtained by highly contestable methods in a number of military trials helped to strengthen this line of argument. In the light of the acts constituting a war crime and a crime against peace and humanity — first listed in the statute to the London Agreement of 8 August 1945 and finally in the provisions of Control Council Law No. 10 relevant for German courts conducting Nazi trials — people spoke of an infringement of the fundamental legal maxim "nullum crimen sine lege" [4]. In so doing, they sometimes overlooked the fact that virtually all the acts described as war crimes and crimes against humanity should have been prosecuted as murder, manslaughter, grievous bodily harm, false imprisonment, duress, larceny and blackmail pursuant to the penal laws in force both then and now [5].

During those years, a parallel movement to the efforts undertaken by the departments of public prosecution and the courts in investigating and punishing Nazi crimes was the activities of the "denazification" authorities, i.e. the Spruchkammer and the Spruchgericht. In line with the instructions of the occupation forces, the various Länder had issued similarly worded laws on "liberation from national socialism and militarism". This legislation stipulated that the political and social record of every adult German citizen should be examined in order to establish whether and, if so, to what extent he had engaged in Nazi activities. To begin with, the operation was carried out with the help of a lengthy questionnaire (comprising no fewer than 131 questions in the American Zone of Occupation, for example). The idea was that it would enable a preliminary decision to be taken on the extent of individual guilt. If certain preconditions — named in the law — were fulfilled, the denazification courts and tribunals classified "those concerned" into one of the following categories: exonerated, follower only, lesser offender,

offender and major offender. Apart from the group of exonerated persons, classification in one of the above-named groups incurred appropriate penalties. These ranged from the imposition of a fine to a committal order for confinement in a labour camp for a maximum period of ten years and a ban on practising one's profession for several years. The fact that a person had belonged to a Nazi organization in some function or other provided sufficient prima facie evidence to incriminate him. The onus of proving that appearances were deceptive rested on his shoulders.

The denazification process, which had commenced in an atmosphere of great seriousness, soon became more and more discredited when it emerged that neither the proceedings per se nor the bodies entrusted with their implementation were able to cope with the great demands made of them. Nazi officials who had perpetrated the most abominable iniquities during the War in the countries occupied by the German army for a certain period of time and who naturally passed over these deeds in silence when completing the questionnaire usually came through the denazification procedure relatively unscathed. Even in cases where involvement in criminal acts such as the murder of Jews in an extermination camp came to light during the proceedings, the denazification courts inflicted relatively light sentences because of the then inadequate knowledge of the background and contemporary events and their inability to discern the gravity and scale of the crimes perpetrated because of the lack of investigatory facilities. On the other hand, severe sentences were often handed down to nominal party members who, in compliance with the urgings of their superiors, had joined the Nazi Party or one of its affiliated organizations and occupied minor "honorary positions" simply in order to protect their families and to retain their jobs. The forging of questionnaires and the granting of the whitewashing "Persilscheine" became as familiar an occurrence as denunciations. The fact that these favours or denunciations were frequently motivated by profiteering, business rivalry or personal animosity rather than political conviction rendered the whole affair even more dubious.

When the denazification courts and tribunals completed their activities in the first half of the 1950s, they could claim to have passed sentences ranging from fines to terms of several years imprisonment on over one and a half million people in the three Western Zones of Occupation alone. None the less, the denazification procedure — fiercely criticized as it was for the above-described reasons as well as others — had been largely instrumental in producing a situation where large segments of German public opinion adopted a reserved and indeed censorious attitude towards the trials conducted not only by the tribunals of the occupying powers, but also by the German courts and prosecuting authorities in connection with the crimes committed during the Nazi régime. Many people held the erroneous view — and apparently still hold it today — that the trials by German courts merely represented a continuation of denazification under another name. Despite these adverse circumstances, the criminal proceedings instituted against a total of 5,228 persons by the German prosecuting authorities in the Federal Republic of Germany up to the end of 1950, notably in pursuance of information furnished by persons who had suffered during the Nazi régime, resulted in the sentencing of those responsible. The fact that their acts mostly involved less grave crimes may be seen from the small number (only 100) of sentences of the first instance inflicted for murder and manslaughter[7].

II 1951—1955

The 1st January 1950 saw the entry into force of Allied High Control Council Law No. 13 on jurisdiction in the reserved areas[8]. Article 1 of this law governing the non-jurisdiction of German courts for certain criminal acts made no reference to Nazi crimes of violence including even those perpetrated against members of Allied nations. Furthermore, Article 14 of the Law put Control Council Law No. 4[9] "out of operation". Nevertheless, Control Council Law No. 10 remained valid (until 1955).

The assumption after 1950 was that German courts would in future be able to prosecute Nazi crimes committed against nationals of Allied countries pursuant to the provisions of German penal law, but that they would not be allowed to apply Control Council Law No. 10. According to statistics provided by the Federal Ministry of Justice, German courts handed down 730 sentences from 1950 to 1951 on the basis of Control Council Law No. 10 in legal proceedings involving Nazi crimes against German nationals or stateless persons. On 31 August 1951, Ordinance No. 234 of the British Military Government and Ordinance No. 171 of the French Military Government cancelled the general powers granted under Article III, para 10 of Control Council Law No. 10 and in consequence German courts could in future only pass judgment in accordance with the provisions of German penal law[10].

Article 103 of the Basic Law of the Federal Republic of Germany contains the principle embodied in every constitution that "an act can be punished only if it was an offence against the law before the act was committed". This principle is set out in Article 1 of the Penal Code. Article 2 lays down that the manner and the severity of the punishment and its secondary consequences shall be governed by the legislation in force at the time when the offence was perpetrated. If the law has been amended during the interval between the commission of the act and the passing of sentence, the least severe punishment shall be imposed.

Among the acts committed during the Third Reich and deemed to be a product of, or closely connected with the

40

Nazi reign of terror and moreover liable to punishment pursuant to both the then and currently valid law, particular mention may be made of the following:

— murder (Article 211 of the Penal Code), liable at the time of commission to the death penalty but since the coming into force of the Basic Law of the Federal Republic of Germany to life-long imprisonment;

— homicide in particularly aggravated circumstances (Art. 212, para 2 of the Penal Code), liable to life-long imprisonment[11];

— Manslaughter (Art. 212, para 1 of the Penal Code), bodily harm with fatal consequences (Art. 226 of the Penal Code) and unlawful detention with fatal consequences (Art. 239, para 3 of the Penal Code) as well as petty and grand larceny (Arts. 249 and 250 of the Penal Code) — liable to a maximum term of 15 years imprisonment;

— bodily harm with malice prepense (Art. 225 of the Penal Code) and unlawful detention for more than one week (Art. 239, para 2 of the Penal Code), liable to a maximum term of 10 years imprisonment;

— other types of bodily harm, unlawful detention and duress, liable to shorter terms of imprisonment not exceeding a maximum of 5 years.

The layman often finds difficulty in distinguishing between murder and manslaughter where substantial importance attaches to the difference not only in respect of the severity of punishment but also in regard to the period of limitation[12]. The relevant provisions of the Penal Code read as follows:

Article 211 Murder
(1) A murderer shall be punished by imprisonment for life.
(2) A murderer is a person who kills another person from thirst for blood, satisfaction of his sexual desires, avarice or other base motives in a malicious or brutal

41

manner or one dangerous to public safety or in order to permit the commission or concealment of another criminal act [13].

Article 212 Manslaughter
(1) Anyone who kills a person without being a murderer shall be punished as a manslayer by a term of five years imprisonment.
(2) In particularly grave cases, a term of imprisonment for life shall be imposed.

Of the characteristics named in Article 211 as indicating a particularly reprehensible killing, it is virtually only the criteria thirst for blood, base motives, maliciousness and brutality which come into question in connection with the prosecuting of nazi crimes. The criterion "thirst for blood" is applied to someone who has killed a person from an abnormal pleasure in destroying human life [14]. Motives are deemed to have been "base" when they are abominable and beneath contempt in the general ethical view as the reason for killing someone [15]. Base motives are above all racial hatred [16] or where the murderer has made himself lord over life and death in an act of sheer despotism [17]. A finding of "malicious" killing presupposes that the criminal exploited the innocence and defencelessness of the victim or victims to perpetrate his deed [18]. A "brutal" murderer is one who inflicts pain or torture on his victims out of lack of feeling or pity [19]. For the purposes of the law, "brutal" is also applied to a mass shooting at which the next victims were able directly to witness the killing of the previous group [20]. On the other hand, a shooting of persons in the form customary in the execution of court-martial sentences is not deemed brutal [21].

Nearly all the judgments pronounced by the jury courts in cases involving Nazi crimes indicated that those principally responsible for the crimes were Hitler, Himmler, Heydrich and other persons at that time holding senior positions of command. As regards those in subordinate positions responsible for carrying out the deeds, the

42

courts had to decide whether these persons should be deemed the accomplices of the above-mentioned principal agents or merely as their accessories, i.e. assistants in crime. The idea at the heart of the judgments handed down by the Federal Supreme Court in this matter was that the main consideration should be the interest shown in the accomplishment of the deed. Anyone who fulfilled the legal characteristics of murder by virtue of his action but thereby completely obeyed the wishes of a third party without taking any interest in the accomplishment of the crime was held to be an accessory and not an accomplice. The German Federal Supreme Court described the following delimitation between the commission of a crime and aiding and abetting in the commission of a crime in the "Stashinski judgment" of 19 October 1962:

> "A person cannot claim to have merely acted as an assistant to his superior in the commission of a crime if he willingly complies with political incitement to commit murder, reduces his conscience to silence and makes the criminal designs of another party the basis of his own convictions and actions or if he ensures within his sphere of influence and duty that such commands are carried out without reserve or if he evinces an approving zeal or exploits such murderous state-terror for his own purposes. The thoughts and acts of such a person are identical with those of the authors of the crime. He is a criminal in the regular sense of the term [22].

In keeping with the judgments pronounced by the Supreme Federal Court in cases involving Nazi crimes, the jury-courts often punished persons accused of aiding and abetting murder where they had in fact objectively committed an act of murder pursuant to Art. 211 of the Penal Code by virtue of their action but where the courts were unable to prove that they had been actuated by their own wishes [23].

In the years 1948 and 1949, the number of successfully completed proceedings reached a climax with 1,819 and

1,523 legally binding convictions. This total dropped rapidly during the next few years until 1955 when only 21 non-appealable sentences, including one case of imprisonment for life, were recorded. This reduction may be explained in part by the limitation commencing in 1950 of the prosecution of all less serious crimes liable to a maximum punishment of five years imprisonment [24].

In addition, there was a sharp fall in the number of denunciations made to the prosecuting authorities subsequent to 1950. After the War, a large number of the preliminary investigations and criminal proceedings were set in train on the strength of information furnished by former inmates of Nazi camps. Since many of the latter had emigrated abroad by the year 1950 and others were fully engaged in trying to make a livelihood for themselves following the Currency Reform of 1948, the interest displayed by this category of persons in bringing Nazi criminals to trial apparently started to wane.

Even though the restrictions placed on German judicial authorities by the Allies had largely been cancelled by 1950, little official action was taken to institute preliminary proceedings. As a rule, the public prosecutors were kept busy with the investigation of everyday crime to the limit of their capacity. If one of them learnt via the Press or the voluminous "concentration camp literature" of those times or — quite apart from the formal preferring of charges — from other sources of the crimes committed in, for example, Poland or Russia, he saw no reason for taking official steps. The scene of the crime lay outside his area of jurisdiction and there was nothing to indicate that the — mostly unknown — perpetrators of the crimes might be living in his particular district. Furthermore, many a theoretically promising case which had been initiated was discontinued at the time because the competent public prosecutor often lacked the background knowledge of contemporary events needed to investigate a Nazi crime and simply capitulated when faced by the apparently unconquerable mountain of difficulties in adducing evidence. When confronted with an investigating officer or public prosecutor unfamiliar with the organizational set-up and the chain of command in the police force existing at the time of the crime, the defendant was often able simply to deny the charges levelled against him and bring about a suspension of proceedings due to lack of evidence. This was facilitated by the fact that many of the accusations appeared to be so incredible as to make it difficult for any right-minded person to believe that such things could possibly have happened.

The beginning of the 1950s saw the end of the denazification proceedings. On 11 May 1951, there entered into force the "Law to settle the Legal Status of Persons falling within the Provisions of Article 131 of the Basic Law"[25]. As a result, many members of the civil service who had been removed from office after the War and not reinstated because of their incrimination in denazification proceedings were now informed — if such incrimination was not too serious — that they could return to their former positions, though usually with a lower rank.

At the same time, the Allies began to reduce the sentences pronounced by their military tribunals against Germans[26] and finally to pardon the convicted. By the middle of the 1950s, those persons were also set free who had originally been condemned to death by Western military tribunals but whose sentence had later been commuted to imprisonment for life and then a short time afterwards to a smaller term of imprisonment before being finally released and bound over on probation[27].

The conclusion of the denazification proceedings, the partial reinstatement of officials removed from office in 1945, the release of Nazi criminals sentenced to very severe punishment by American, British and French occupation authorities and finally the efforts undertaken to establish armed forces in the Federal Republic of Germany created the impression in public that the goal of "coming to terms with the past had now been reached". The opinion prevailed in wide sections of the population that those responsible for Nazi crimes who had survived the War and not succeeded in disappearing abroad had now been tracked down and called to account by the courts of the victorious Allies or the German judicial authorities and denazification bodies.

Although the number of preliminary investigations rose again slightly after 1953, the cause of this probably lay in the coming into force of the "Federal Supplementary Law for the Compensation of the Victims of Nazi Persecution" of 18 September 1953[28]. A large number of persecutees of the Nazi régime who had been living abroad and whose whereabouts had hitherto not been known to the public authorities in the Federal Republic of Germany now came forward with a claim for compensation. These compensation procedures brought to light new crimes, which had not been investigated by the public prosecutors. In addition, literature on this subject provided fresh clues. Nevertheless, there was no noticeable increase in the prosecution of Nazi crimes.

By the end of 1955, a total of 5,866 persons had been sentenced by German courts since the War for their involvement in Nazi crimes. The Spring of 1955 marked the commencement of limitation on such crimes as were liable in law to a maximum term of imprisonment of 10 years[29]. The significance of this was that in future only wilful homicide could be prosecuted.

At the same time (5. 5. 1955), there entered into force the "Convention on the Settlement of Matters arising from the War and Occupation" — sometimes called the Transition Agreement — concluded between the USA, Great Britain, France and the Federal Republic of Germany and also Allied High Commission Law No. A-37 on the termination of the validity and the annulment of certain provisions of occupation law [30]. This virtually brought to an end the remaining restrictions in the field of criminal legislation placed on the German legal authorities. There was however a significant exception in Article 3, paragraph 3b of the Transition Agreement which provided that German courts were allowed to exercise the jurisdiction vested in them pursuant to German law

> ". . . in criminal proceedings against natural persons, **unless** investigation of the alleged offence was finally completed by the prosecuting authorities of the Power or Powers concerned, or unless such offence has been committed in the performance of duties or services for the Occupation authorities".

This clause exercised an immense psychological effect on the Nazi trials held at a later stage by German courts. High-ranking Nazi officials who had been investigated by British, French or American prosecuting authorities for certain offences but whose cases were dismissed due to lack of evidence could not be brought to trial today even if one adduced proof of their guilt. The former commanders of Security Police and Security Service operational groups and units, sentenced by the American military tribunal in Nuremberg in the "operational unit trial" but later pardoned, had all been released by the middle of the 1950s (at the latest by 1958) and could no longer be called to account. On the other hand, their former subordinates were put on trial in the following years and in many cases sentenced to imprisonment for life.

III 1956—1964

The year 1956 marked the start of fresh developments. As a result of the agreements concluded during the visit of the then Federal Chancellor Adenauer to Moscow, several thousand German prisoners of war returned home

47

from the Soviet Union that year. Among those not covered by the amnesty were some who had been wanted for some time by the German prosecuting authorities because of crimes committed in Nazi concentration camps[31]. Others came forward as witnesses and thus helped to furnish a significant contribution towards clearing up certain series of crimes whose full range had not hitherto been perceived.

Yet the main impetus for intensifying and concentrating the prosecution of Nazi crimes came from a trial which had been initiated more or less by chance. A former SS officer and chief of police in Memel in 1941 had been put in charge of a refugee camp after the War while living under an assumed name and after having been exonerated in denazification proceedings. When his real identity became known, he was dismissed whereupon he took legal action to be reinstated in the civil service. When the Press reported the case, one reader remembered that the man in question had played a leading part in the mass execution of Jews in the border area between Germany and Lithuania during the opening phase of the Russian campaign in June 1941. In 1956, the man was arrested.

The wide-ranging and meticulous investigations set in motion by his arrest and culminating in the "Ulm operational unit trial" revealed beyond doubt that many of the gravest Nazi crimes, notably those perpetrated in the East, had not yet been punished at all. In accordance with a suggestion made by the Ministry of Justice in Baden-Württemberg with the original impetus coming from the Director of Public Prosecutions at the Regional Court of Appeal in Stuttgart responsible for the area within whose jurisdiction the case of the Ulm operational groups fell, the Länder Ministers and Senators of Justice decided during their conference at Bad Harzburg in October 1958 to set up a Central Office of the Land Judicial Authorities for the Investigation of National-Socialist Crimes ("Zentrale Stelle der Landesjustizverwaltungen zur Aufklärung nationalsozialistischer Verbrechen"). The permanent seat for this central agency, whose staff and facilities are funded by all the federal Länder, is Ludwigsburg near Stuttgart — chosen because suitable office accommodation could be provided there at short notice[33].

In pursuance of the administrative agreement reached by the Ministers and Senators of Justice, the terms of reference of the Central Office were — to begin with — confined to investigating Nazi killings for which the scene of the crime did not provide any jurisdiction within federal territory and which had moreover been committed against civilians during World War II beyond the ambit of military action[34]. The main targets were the crimes of murder and manslaughter carried out by the operational groups and units of Security Police and Security Service men as well as those perpetrated in concentration and labour camps or in the ghettos. Hence, the Central Office did not initially possess any jurisdiction to investigate the killing of prisoners in concentration camps located on the territory of what today constitutes the Federal Republic of Germany. Above all, the Central Office was not to have competence, either, for investigating genuine war crimes inasmuch as they were not inseparably linked with criminal acts inspired by a Nazi mentality[35]. These proceedings were in fact to be conducted exclusively by the public prosecutors, competent to do so by virtue of the (principal) defendant's place of residence or the place of the crime, without any prior intervention by the Central Office.

A special feature was the inquiry into the liability in criminal law of members of the Reich Security Office. Although the immediate effects of the latter's activities made themselves felt in the remotest corners of the territories occupied by the German army, it was decided in the interest of centralizing the preliminary proceedings against members of the Reich Security Office to entrust the public prosecutor at Berlin Superior Court of Justice (Kammergericht) with all cases, since Berlin had also been the scene of the crime.

The mandate for the Central Office pursuant to the Administrative Agreement states that it should collect and sift all the relevant records obtainable about the criminal acts under investigation and that it should separate delimitable series of crimes and determine the whereabouts of the perpetrators. The facts ascertained in the course of these preliminary inquiries must then be transmitted to the public prosecutor with local jurisdiction for the (principal) defendant's place of residence or domicile so that he can institute formal preliminary proceedings. As the Central Office itself is not a department of public prosecution pursuant to the wishes of its constituent members, it cannot prefer charges. Nor can it obtain permission from a court to examine and seize property or apply for a warrant of arrest. If the inquiries carried out by the Central Office indicate the necessity of such a step, the action can nevertheless only be taken by a public prosecutor.

In its implementation of these judicial inquiries, the Central Office receives the support of the local criminal police departments and notably the special commissions set up at each Land Criminal Police Office.

The terms of reference given to the Central Office produced almost a reversal of the former procedure adopted in the prosecution of Nazi crimes. The investigations were no longer set in motion by the laying of information about a suspect — and only then — as had so far been the rule in the past: instead, certain pointers to a crime still liable to prosecution triggered the preliminary proceedings against person or persons unknown or not yet traced. The question as to the competence of a public prosecutor's office (and the failure to provide an answer to this had occasionally thwarted the institution of proceedings) no longer arose at the commencement of the investigations, but at a point of time when the facts of the case had been broadly cleared up with the resulting detection of at least one suspect.

The Central Office performs at least one other function under the terms of the Administrative Agreement. Public prosecutors are obliged to forward to the Central Office all the findings which they obtain during the proceedings and set out in the minutes of the examination sessions as well as in other documents together with their concluding notes. This also applies to notification of legal measures and decisions pronounced during the proceedings. The registration of these data in a card-index permits the Central Office to coordinate the preliminary and criminal proceedings pending before the courts and public prosecutor's offices and thus avoid superfluous duplication of investigations as much as possible [36].

On 1 December 1958, i.e. only a few weeks after the Ministers and Senators of Justice had taken their decision, the Central Office in Ludwigsburg commenced its activities and by the end of the month it had already initiated 64 judicial inquiries. Following a fairly rapid solution of the customary incipient problems attendant upon the organization of a new department and the gradual arrival of the staff seconded to the Central Office from the various federal Länder, a start was made in mid-1959 on apportioning the work on a regional basis. The significance of this consisted in the provision of a specified person to handle the affairs of the various localities (such as the old Reich districts of Danzig West-Prussia and Wartheland; the "Generalgouvernement"; North, Central and South Russia etc.). This enabled the staff concerned to acquire the expert skill and knowledge about the officials and policemen actively engaged in that area and moreover about their chain of command. A short time later, one member of the Central Office was appointed to examine all convincingly described cases where the defendant had pleaded superior orders.

During the first weeks and months of the Central Office's activities, the only source of information normally available for use was the relevant literature (including the official publications on the trials held at the International Military Tribunal in Nuremberg — the "blue books") plus the files on past criminal proceedings in this field. The reports disseminated in the Press on the setting up of the Central Office in Ludwigsburg resulted in the receipt of clues from various circles as to where further material might be found.

In 1959, the Central Office initiated 400 judicial inquiries. The major cases concerned the crimes committed by the operational groups and units of the Security Police and Security Service in Russia and in the extermination camps of Auschwitz, Belzec, Sobibor, Treblinka and Chelmno.

In spring 1960, the general public became really aware for the first time of the problem inherent in the limitation of Nazi crimes of violence.

Limitation rules out judicial punishment of a criminal act. With the exception of an act of genocide — first incorporated within the Penal Code of the Federal Republic of Germany in 1954 (Article 220a) but inapplicable to Nazi crimes because of the prohibition on retroactive legislation — all crimes become statute-barred after a certain period of time has expired.

Pursuant to Article 67 of the Penal Code (in the valid version operative until the coming into force of the "9th Law to Amend the Penal Code" of 6 August 1969), the limitation of crimes liable to a life sentence was 20 years; for criminal acts liable to a term of imprisonment of more than ten years, a period of 15 years; and for other criminal acts, 10 years.

As a rule, these periods commence upon the completion of the criminal act. Crimes which today come under the heading of Nazi crimes were not however prosecuted during the time of the "Third Reich" as they conformed with the system then in force. True, some public prosecutors had attempted during the early stages of the Nazi régime to conduct investigations about the persons responsible for such crimes. Yet, with few exceptions, these efforts met with failure: the proceedings were quashed in compliance with categorical orders received from above. Pursuant to Art. 69 of the Penal Code, a limitation is interrupted during times when criminal prosecution cannot be initiated or continued because of certain legal provisions. In keeping with the legal concept behind this rule, there was a suspension of limitation until the end of the War in all those cases where the "will of the führer" (which was deemed to be law) objectively barred prosecution[37].

Furthermore, the various zones of occupation enacted special laws which prescribed the interrupting of limitation until 8 May 1945 and in some cases for a short time thereafter[38].

The limitation in respect of bodily harm, unlawful detention and offences against property[39] committed during the Nazi era and punishable by a maximum sentence of ten years imprisonment commenced ten years after the end of the War, i.e. as a rule on 8 May 1955. Manslaughter, bodily harm with fatal consequences and robbery became statute-barred after 15 years, i.e. 8 May 1960.

The mandatory rule up to the coming into force of the Ordinance of 5 December 1939[40] had been for the handing down of less severe sentences to accessories than to the perpetrator himself. This meant that the aiding and abetting of a Nazi murder occurring prior to the above-mentioned date (i.e. during the first three months of the War) was only liable to a maximum penalty of 15 years imprisonment and thus also statute-barred as from 8 May 1960.

A draft law, presented by the SPD parliamentary party on 23 March 1960 on computing the periods of limitation in criminal law and aimed at extending by four years the start of limitation, was rejected by the Bundestag[41]. As a result, any killings qualified as manslaughter as well as the crime of aiding and abetting murder committed prior to 5 December 1939 could no longer be prosecuted unless limitation had been interrupted in the meantime[42].

For the crime of murder committed in connection with the Nazi régime and liable to life imprisonment, the period of limitation under the then valid legal provisions was not due to expire until five years later, i.e. on 8 May 1965. As it could not yet be seen in the proceedings pending with the Central Office and the public prosecutor's offices whether the subject of their investigations would finally prove to be murder or manslaughter, an effort was made to meet all contingencies by preventing the inception of limitation for the crime of manslaughter, too, and to use every available legal device to achieve this end.

The law provides an opportunity for averting the commencement of limitation by means of periods of interruption. The relevant provisions as set out in the version valid as of 31 December 1974 (Article 69 of the Penal Code) read as follow:

(1) Any act undertaken by the judge against the perpetrator of a crime shall be deemed to interrupt the limitation.

(2) Such interruption shall only operate against the person to whom the said act applies.

(3) When the interruption terminates, a new limitation shall commence.

A short time prior to the expiry of the limitation period in respect of manslaughter, the Main Polish Commission for the Investigation of Nazi Crimes set up at the Ministry of Justice in Warsaw (the "Main Commission") forward-ed the Central Office in Ludwigsburg via the Polish Military Mission in Berlin a set of documents that resulted in a large number of initial inquiries. In order to avert the danger of the crimes becoming statute-barred, the Central Office provided the Attorney General with records showing that hitherto the whereabouts of none of the accused could be ascertained with a resulting absence of local jurisdiction for any public prosecutor within the Federal Republic of Germany. The Central Office suggested that the Attorney General should ask the Federal Supreme Court to establish jurisdiction in pursuance of Article 13a of the Code of Criminal Procedure. When this jurisdiction had been established, it proved possible to interrupt the limitation on prosecuting hundreds of suspects whose exact identity was not yet known. In addition, the public prosecutors had in many cases arranged for witnesses to be questioned by the judges and for them to be shown lists of accused persons and asked what they knew about the latter. In this way, the period of limitation was interrupted in numerous cases in respect of those suspects already discovered and also those named and adequately identified but not yet traced.

In the summer of 1960, the then Head of the Central Office and two of his staff were given an opportunity to spend several weeks in the American national archives — World War II Records Division — at Alexandria near Washington in order to evaluate German records and files taken by American officials to the USA upon the completion of the military tribunal trials in Germany. The documents which the German team selected and submitted to the Central Office in the form of authenticated film copies provided numerous clues to Nazi crimes which had not yet been prosecuted under criminal law. At the time, the Federal Government did not take up another suggestion, i.e. that it should contact the Eastern states (and in particular Poland) with a view to evaluating the sets of documents stored in the archives there[43].

In 1963, Poland forwarded more documentary material via its military mission in Berlin. At about the same time, two Soviet officials attending a hearing at a Nazi trial in Coblence brought with them a large number of original documents, which they then presented to the Federal Archives located in the same town for the purpose of making photostats. However, these initial contacts were not pursued any further due to the above-mentioned attitude adopted by the Federal Government. On the other hand, a member of the staff at the Central Office in Ludwigsburg was given access to relevant files stored in Brussels.

Despite the fairly modest size of the staff available to the Central Office between 1959 and 1964 (a total of 20 to 25 persons including, on an average, 8 to 10 public prosecutors and judges), judicial inquiries were initiated during that period in respect of all the major series of crimes falling within the substantive jurisdiction of the Office (crimes committed by Security Police operational groups and Self-Protection Units of the ethnic Germans in Poland; the crimes of the Security Police and Security Service operational groups in the USSR; crimes committed in connection with the "final solution" of the Jewish question; crimes in concentration camps not located on the territory of the Federal Republic of Germany; crimes in "euthanasia centres"; crimes perpetrated against prisoners of war). Where the crimes concerned events based on standard orders from supreme governmental and police agencies applicable throughout their entire orbit of power (and thus analagous to the measures taken in conjunction with the "final solution" of the Jewish question), the Central Office also instituted proceedings in regard to those geographic areas for which there was not yet any concrete reference to the crimes committed there. At the same time, a comprehensive range of investigations were undertaken by a large staff at the Chief State Prosecutor's office at the Superior Court of Justice (Kammergericht) in Berlin. A systematic analysis was also made of documentary evidence in those archives thought to contain relevant material such as the Bavarian State Archives in Nuremberg, the Federal Archives in Coblence, the Federal (Military) Archives in Freiburg, the Federal Archives Registry in Kornelimünster, the "German Office for informing the Next-of-Kin of former Wehrmacht Soldiers killed in Action" (WA st) in Berlin, the Document Center of the US Mission in Berlin, the Institute for Contemporary History in Munich, the Red Cross International Tracing Service in Arolsen, the Federal Armed Forces Research Department for Military History in Freiburg, the Political Archives of the Federal Foreign Office plus a number of Land Archives and Depots containing compensation and restitution records [44].

From the inception of its activities on 1 December 1958 until the end of 1964, the Central Office in Ludwigsburg initiated 701 judicial inquiries with 545 of them then going to public prosecutors throughout the Federal Republic of Germany so as to permit the institution of formal preliminary proceedings in criminal law. (Similarly, it proved possible to link up 93 other judicial inquiries with cases already in progress). As a result of the mostly systematic investigation of Nazi crimes after 1959, a substantial increase also took place in the number of jury-court proceedings conducted after 1960. On an average, there were only 13 per year between 1956 and 1959 compared with 21 between 1960 and 1965.

IV 1965—1970

On 20 November 1964, i.e. less than six months before the commencement of limitation for Nazi killings on 8 May 1965 pursuant to the then valid legislation, the

Federal Government directed a proclamation to all states and individuals to come forward with any hitherto unknown documentary evidence on Nazi crimes which they might have in their possession[45]. As the proclamation expressly pointed out, the Federal Government assumed at the time that it would not prove possible for constitutional reasons to extend the period of limitation beyond 9 May 1965. The German Bundestag associated itself with this plea by the Federal Government on 9 December 1964 and moreover authorized it to commence negotiations without delay with the Länder governments with the aim of reaching an agreement on the following points:

1. A systematic analysis to be made of the whole range of documentary evidence on murders committed during the Nazi era.
2. An extension of the analysis to embrace all documentary material to the extent that
   a) it is available on the territory of the Federal Republic of Germany and not yet completely sifted;
   b) obtainable from the archives of the Soviet Zone of Occupation; or
   c) obtainable from abroad and in particular from East European countries.
3. The systematic analysis will be carried out by a central department of the Länder judicial authorities. Irrespective of the locality where the crime was committed, this department will be competent to examine all murders including incitement or aiding and abetting in the commission of murder within the purview of the authorities and agencies of the former Reich Government and central Nazi organizations.

A meeting held two days later on 11 December 1964 between the Federal Minister of Justice and the Minister or Senators of Justice from nine Länder produced unanimous agreement on the first two points. However, point 3 of the declaration was amended to read as follows:

"The systematic analysis of documents shall be entrusted to the Central Office of the Land Judicial Authorities for

the Investigation of National-Socialist Crimes in Ludwigsburg.

Its jurisdiction shall extend to crimes committed on German territory with the exception of those falling under the
heading of the Reich Security Office (which remain within
the jurisdiction of the chief state prosecutor at the Supreme Court of Justice in Berlin) and also those cases already pending with the public prosecutor's offices.

The personnel at the Central Office shall be augmented in
order to assist it in the implementation of its additional
tasks.

The Central Office shall immediately contact the Polish
authorities with a view to evaluating the documents held
by the Poles".

A week later, talks were held in the Ministry of Justice in
Warsaw between representatives from the Main Polish
Commission and the Central Office in Ludwigsburg to
discuss the procedure for evaluating the documentary evidence stored in Polish archives. Under the agreement
then reached, a team of public prosecutors from the Central Office were able to spend a period of four weeks as
from the beginning of February 1965 studying the documents submitted to them at the Polish Ministry of Justice
and the Institute of Jewish History in Warsaw. The results confirmed the assumption that the Polish archives
housed immense quantities of evidence on crimes which
had hitherto not been prosecuted. Moreover, they revealed with sobering explicitness the unrealistic nature of the
Federal Government's plan set out in its declaration of
20 November 1964 that the large volume of documents
provided by foreign countries could be processed by
8 May 1965 to such an extent as to bring about a timely
interruption in the limitation of at least the bulk of Nazi
murders listed in such evidence.

The voluminous information furnished by individuals in
response to the Federal Government's declaration only
resulted in the initiation of a handful of new proceedings.

59

Most of the information comprised reports of a general nature or denunciations apparently inspired by personal enmity. A number of countries transmitted a substantial amount of material. However, it could not have been analyzed in time to permit the interruption of limitation on suspected crimes before the final date of 8 May 1965. A particularly useful item was a set of photocopied documents (comprising only 643 pages to begin with) presented in February 1965 by a representative from the Association of Czechoslovakian Anti-Fascist Resistance Fighters and taken from the State Archives in Prague. They formed part of a series of documents reported by the Press to have been recovered a few months previously from a container apparently discovered by chance in a lake in Czechoslovakia[46].

In February 1965, the Federal Minister of Justice forwarded the Bundestag a report on the prosecution of Nazi crimes[46a]. The report indicated the possibility that major undetected crimes or unknown criminals holding senior positions might still be revealed after 8 May 1965.

A motion tabled in January 1965 by Herr Benda M. P. and other CDU members of parliament designed to extend the limitation for crimes liable to life imprisonment to 30 years was amended after presentation of the abovementioned report to the effect that such crimes should not be subject to any limitation[46b]. At the same time, the SPD parliamentary party submitted two draft laws providing for the non-prescription of murder and genocide and an appropriate amplification of the Basic Law[47]. On the strength of these bills, the "Statute on computing Periods of Limitation in Criminal Law" was voted by the Bundestag on 25 March 1965 after two lengthy debates[48]. The new Act decreed the exclusion of the period from 8 May 1945 to 31 December 1949 from any computation of the period of limitation for the prosecution of crimes liable to life imprisonment. In consequence, the period of limitation for Nazi murders could not expire before 31 December 1969. In order to meet all eventualities, the agencies concerned with the prosecution of Nazi crimes had arranged — similar to the situation in 1960 during the weeks and months prior to the Bundestag vote — to direct the courts to interrupt limitation in numerous cases where the perpetrators were known by name or individually identifiable, but not yet traced.

Following a resolution adopted by the Land Ministers and Senators of Justice on 28 April 1965, the Central Office substantially augmented its staff and facilities in the course of the following two years. In 1968 and 1969, 121 persons including 48 judges or public prosecutors were seconded to the Office. At that time, a total of 200 public prosecutors and examining judges plus the same number of criminal investigation officers were simultaneously and exclusively engaged in investigating and prosecuting Nazi crimes, i.e. in addition to the members of the Central Office and the denazification tribunals handling their own cases. These totals gradually sank in the course of the next few years.

The years 1967 to 1969 saw a sharp rise in the volume of documents provided by public authorities abroad for use by the criminal prosecution bodies in the Federal Republic of Germany [49]. In 1965 and 1966, representatives of the Central Office travelled to Poland and Czechoslovakia and in some cases spent weeks there evaluating documents in the archives. In Autumn 1968, the Soviet Union acceded to a request from the Federal Government that members of the Central Office should be allowed to analyze documents kept at the Central Archives in Moscow. They were also able to examine sets of documents in France, Belgium, the Netherlands, Luxemburg, Austria, Norway, England and Israel. In many cases, the personnel and examining judges concerned with investigations in public prosecutors' offices and courts went abroad to question witnesses and sift documents.

The German consulates, notably in the USA, Canada and Australia as well as elsewhere, provided substantial investigatory and legal assistance by questioning witnesses on the spot. It mostly proved to be an arduous and time-consuming task to trace the addresses of these persons and it was often only possible with the help of the secretariat of the World Jewish Congress in New York. At the same time, the Investigating Department for Nazi Crimes at the National Office of the Israeli Police forwarded a large number of files containing the minutes of witnesses' evidence on certain series of crimes. The Head of the Documentation Centre for Jewish Persecutees under the Nazi Régime in Vienna, Simon Wiesenthal, also submitted the information sent to him from all over the world on Nazi crimes and on the known or presumed whereabouts of criminals.

The bulk of the documents traced during the analysis of archive items and other evidence furnished to the prosecuting authorities was put to use in pending trials, although much of it merely served as background material. At the same time, the faster flow of information produced a sharp rise in the number of judicial inquiries initiated by the Central Office and a little later a concomitant rise in the preliminary proceedings emanating from the public prosecutors.

A major part of the information leading to the institution of new proceedings came from the ranks of criminals themselves. The questioning by the police, public prosecutors and judges of former members of the Security Police, Security Service and other organizations significantly involved in the crimes provided a continuous stream of clues which helped to clear up criminal acts hitherto not prosecuted.

Alone in the year 1967, a total of 436 judicial inquiries were set in train by Ludwigsburg. Apart from a few exceptions, the new proceedings did not however match the major series of crimes tackled between 1959 and 1965 either in volume (in terms of victims) or the contemporary response they evoked.

The main brunt of the investigatory activities had long since passed from the Central Office to the public prosecutors. The investigations conducted by Ludwigsburg since 1959 had succeeded within a fairly short space of time in bringing about the detection of persons suspected of having participated in graver series of crimes involving a large number of people and residing within the local jurisdiction of a public prosecutor in the Federal Republic. In these cases, the Central Office had passed on the accumulated evidence without delay to the public prosecutors in order to concentrate on those investigations which arose by virtue of the receipt of fresh material. Henceforth, the Central Office was more concerned to coordinate the proceedings in progress all over the Federal Republic, to provide the public prosecutors with ideas and encouragement and to bring about an exchange of views and experience. Between 1964 and 1970, the Justice Ministry of Baden-Württemberg acting under the aegis of the Central Office organized a series of 5-day working conferences attended in each instance by some 70 to 100 public prosecutors and examining judges engaged in the prosecution of Nazi crimes.

As from 1961, the prosecution of Nazi crimes extensively and systematically carried out since 1959 resulted in an increased number of convictions. Between 1961 and 1968, jury courts of the first instance handed down sentences to 492 persons accused of homicide: 68 were condemned to life imprisonment and 271 to other terms of imprisonment[50].

From 5 December 1939 to 31 December 1974, an accessory in the commission of a murder was liable to the same punishment as the murderer himself.

After the amendment of Article 50 para 2 of the Penal Code on 1 October 1968, however, there came into force a legal provision whereby, subject to certain preconditions, the aiding and abetting of Nazi-inspired murders was deemed to be statute-barred. The new version of Art. 50, para 2 of the Penal Code announced in the introductory law to the Law on Summary Offences[51] reads as follows:

> "Where the accessory lacks special personal characteristics, conditions and circumstances (and in particular personal features) such as establish the criminal nature of the perpetrator, his sentence shall be less severe and determined pursuant to the provisions governing the punishment of an attempted crime".

In its judgment of 20 May 1969, the Federal Supreme Court ruled that a case of "base motives" should be deemed to be a criterion related to the perpetrator of the crime himself within the meaning of Art. 50, para 2 of the Penal Code[52]. Hence, failure to prove that a person who had taken part in a murder committed for reasons of racial hatred was personally motivated by racial hatred meant that he had to be given a mitigated sentence.

As the Federal Supreme Court explained in detail during the judgment in question, this also implied because of the amendment of 1 October 1968 to Article 50, para 2 of the Penal Code with retroactive effect to 8 May 1960 that limitation commenced unless it had previously been interrupted.

After that, an accessory merely acting under orders could only be punished if it was demonstrated that his contribution to the crime sprang from base motives or that he was aware of the cruel or malicious nature of the crime at the time of its commission.

As the Federal Minister of Justice stressed on 11 June 1969 in the Bundestag, the restrictive impact of the amendment to the Law did not accord with the wishes of the law-makers and this aspect had apparently been over-looked during the deliberations on the bill[53]. In consequence, it was no longer possible to bring to trial a number of the "armchair culprits" who had undeniably acted without being principals in the first degree. The main category of persons to benefit from this were the members of the Reich Security Office against whom the Berlin Superior Court of Justice had initiated criminal proceedings. In addition, there were members of other supreme Reich authorities against whom numerous judicial inquiries as well as preliminary and criminal proceedings had been mounted because of their suspected participation in Nazi crimes.

On 26 November 1968, the Convention on the Non-Applicability of the legal Limitation Provisions on War Crimes and Crimes against Humanity[54] was voted by the General Assembly of the United Nations pursuant to a resolution submitted by the United Nations Economic and Social Council[55]. The Convention came into force on 1 November 1970. As Article IV obliged the signatory states to annul retroactively a limitation which had already commenced, the Federal Republic of Germany did not accede to it. In its major debate of 10 March 1965 on limitation, the Bundestag unanimously agreed that a retroactive annulment of a limitation already in force would infringe the Basic Law. The Federal Constitutional Court corroborated this legal view—though for other reasons[56].

V After 1970

Under the Statute on computing Periods of Limitation in Criminal Law, the 20-year period of prescription for Nazi murders commencing on 1 January 1950 was due to expire on 31 December 1969[57]. As in 1960 and 1964, the prosecuting authorities again endeavoured to bring about a judicial interruption of the limitation period in respect of untraced suspects whose exact identity had not yet been determined. It had however meanwhile emerged that the judicial interruption, which would have been feasible in 1964 in certain cases, had not been effected so that limitation would have commenced in 1965 if the deadline had not been postponed until 31 December 1969 by law. In order to prevent delay, the public prosecutors in the Federal Republic engaged in bringing Nazi criminals to trial held a working conference in Freiburg to discuss the organizational measures needed to interrupt limitation. They also discussed those cases in which the culprits were presumed to be living abroad, where the declarations of presumed death pronounced by the courts seemed questionable or where the fate of the culprits deemed to have been killed during the War or to have meanwhile died appeared to be still in doubt. No precise information is available about the scale on which judicial interruptions were obtained in these cases during the following years. According to the Central Office, however, it may be assumed that this occurred in numerous proceedings.

Nevertheless, these preventive measures finally proved — i.e. in relation to 31 December 1969 — to be superfluous[58]. In the event, the Federal Government introduced a bill providing for an annulment of the limitation of murder and genocide. The bill was amended during its readings in the Bundestag. On 26 June 1969, the Bundestag approved by a majority of over two thirds of all votes cast the "9th Law to amend the Penal Code"[59]. The new Law stipulated that the prosecution of crimes liable to life imprisonment would henceforth become statute-barred after 30 years (instead of 20 as previously). The significance of this in regard to murders committed during the Nazi régime lay in the postponement of the start of limitation for

66

those cases which have not been meanwhile interrupted until 31 December 1979.

By about the year 1970, all crimes (with very few exceptions) known to the prosecuting authorities by virtue of documentary proof or the evidence of witnesses had resulted in either pending or completed judicial inquiries and in preliminary or criminal proceedings initiated by the Central Office in Ludwigsburg, the public prosecutors' offices or the courts themselves. During the next few years, the Central Office commenced a relatively large number of fresh judicial inquiries on the strength of previously unknown crimes or those undetected by virtue of their being classified under other pending criminal cases [60]. The main factor in setting these proceedings in train was the documentary evidence arriving in Ludwigsburg at irregular intervals, mainly from Poland but also on a smaller scale from other states. As regards Czechoslovakia, the fairly infrequent consignments of evidence received were invariably well prepared cases with very precise references to individuals and culprits (sometimes with a full statement of personal particulars). Although the numerous files sent by the Main Polish Commission comprising copies of interrogations, photographs, sketches of the scene of the criminal act and copies of documents usually contained quite a precise description of the circumstances of the crime, they seldom provided such clues or references as would permit a swift location and identification of the suspects.

Of the 1,383 judicial inquiries [61] undertaken by the Central Office between 1973 and 1978, a total of 895 cases (i.e. two thirds of the proceedings during the period) rested on fresh information provided at the time by the Main Polish Commission. This information, largely based as it was only on the minutes of the questioning of witnesses, often concerned crimes of which the prosecuting authorities of the Federal Republic had no knowledge due to the lack of appropriate references to them in previous documents and witnesses' statements. The fact that investigations to trace the culprits did not commence until thirty or more years after the commission of the crimes cannot be blamed on the judicial authorities in the Federal Republic.

The content of the information received referred more and more frequently to the killing of non-combatants in 1939 or 1944/45, i.e. in direct connection with the War. Quite often, these cases revealed that the characteristics constituting murder such as brutality, malice, thirst for blood or base motives were lacking in the cases described[62]. The Central Office, whose jurisdiction for the investigating of genuine war crimes is categorically ruled out by virtue of the Administrative Agreement between the Ministers and Senators of Justice, forwards these cases without having made any inquiries of its own (though together with the available evidence) to a competent public prosecutor's office or one declared to be competent by the Federal Supreme Court. For this reason, there has been an increase in recent years in the number of cases where the Central Office, faced with its inability to determine the regional competence of a public prosecutor within the Federal Republic, has forwarded the case to the Attorney General with a request that the Federal Supreme Court itself should stipulate a legal venue pursuant to Article 13a of the Code of Criminal Procedure[63].

The bulk of the preliminary proceedings pending with public prosecutors in the years after 1970 originated from the judicial inquiries made by the Central Office. Nevertheless, numerous proceedings were opened in respect of those crimes whose prosecution had been separated from other (usually major) actions for reasons of procedural economy or the subsequently determined lack of factual relevance.

68

The number of jury-court cases leading to a sentence in the first instance reached its culminating point in 1968 with 30 verdicts (against 118 accused) and then fell steadily during the next few years, i.e. apart from a short-lived rise in 1973. It recorded its hitherto lowest level in 1978 when only four trials against four accused were completed, resulting in four sentences in the first instance[64].

The amended version of the Penal Code entering into force on 1 January 1975 changed the provisions governing the interruption of limitation and this proved to possess great significance in the proceedings involving Nazi crimes. Pursuant to Art. 78c of the Penal Code, persons charged with an offence must at least be informed by the police, the public proscutor's office or the court of the institution of legal action against him or else a court warrant of arrest, commitment, production of prisoner for trial, attachment or search must be obtained. If the whereabouts of a Nazi criminal is not known, the public prosecutor must obtain a judge's order of arrest in order to interrupt the limitation: that, in turn, presupposes sufficient substance to justify the suspicion of a criminal offence[65].

On 9 April 1975, there came into force the "Agreement on German Jurisdiction for the Prosecution of certain Crimes" which had been concluded between Germany and France on 2 February 1971[66]. This accord closed the gap in the chain of prosecution created by the "Transition Agreement". In those cases where a French court handed down a non-enforceable sentence against a non-apprehended German accused in his absence and where the said accused then turned up in the Federal Republic of Germany, the French judicial authorities had been unable to attain his extradition. By the same token, the Transition Agreement prevented the judicial organs of the Federal Republic from prosecuting the person concerned. Under the new Agreement, German courts were now given competence to prosecute in all such cases.

As early as 1965, the Central Office in Ludwigsburg had received lists with 956 cases of German nationals sentenced in their absence by French military tribunals. In 422 instances, the reason named for the judgment was a killing (homicide volontaire, assassinat, meutre, représaille); in 205 cases listed without the reason for the judgment, the sentence imposed (i.e. death) indicates that the crimes involved homicide. The assumption in regard to all the other cases was that the limitation had been interrupted. In addition to the designation of the trial court, the lists also set out the file number of the proceedings, the date of the sentence and the (occasionally phonetically spelt) surname of the accused. In many cases, the Christian name, the date of birth (less frequent), the place of origin and other helpful information facilitating identification were also quoted. Even the very first initial inquiries undertaken by the Central Office revealed that a considerable number of the identifiable persons had died in the meantime.

In keeping with the agreements concluded between the Governments of the Federal Republic of Germany and France, the French authorities permitted public prosecutors from Cologne, Dortmund and Ludwigsburg to pay a series of visits in 1976 to the military tribunals in Paris, Bordeaux, Lyons and Marseilles in order to evaluate the relevant files stored there. As a result of this analysis, the French authorities forwarded in stages over 50,000 pages of photocopied records to the Central Office in Ludwigsburg by the Summer of 1977. One third of this material was sent after a short examination of the contents to the department of public prosecution in Cologne and one third to Dortmund (the central agencies) for use in the numerous preliminary proceedings pending there. The smaller part of the remaining third was forwarded to various public prosecutors engaged in pending actions. By the Summer of 1978, the initial inquiries set in train by the Central Office on the strength of the residual material had reached such an advanced stage as to be transferable to a number of public prosecutors for the commencement of preliminary proceedings in criminal law.

Overall, the documentary evidence sent to the German prosecuting authorities following a study of French military tribunal records has been used in 92 of the preliminary proceedings hitherto instituted by public prosecutors. Some of these criminal proceedings have had to be terminated due to the commencement of limitation, as the killings named in the proceedings do not amount to murder (the only indictable crime under the current law). In the case concerning the transport of Jews from France to the extermination camps in the East, the department (central agency) of public prosecution in Cologne has meanwhile brought charges against former SS officer and deputy-commissioner of the Head of the Security Police and Security Service in France, Kurt Lischka.

As of January 1979, 173 judicial inquiries were in progress at the Central Office. At the present stage of the judicial inquiries, it is impossible to estimate the number of persons deemed to be suspects for the purpose of these proceedings. The proceedings pending with the public prosecutors' offices, i.e. cases which have not been either dismissed or concluded by the pronouncing of sentence, currently involve a total of 2,612 accused persons. As of January 1979, trials were in progress at jury-courts in respect of eleven criminal proceedings. According to information furnished by the Central Office, dates have been arranged for trials in five other criminal proceedings.

D. Trials by Courts in the German Democratic Republic and in East Berlin

A brochure issued by the GDR authorities in January 1965 entitled "The Attitude of the two German States to Nazi and War Crimes" listed the following statistics for the period 1945 to 1964: 12,807 convictions comprising 118 death sentences, 231 life sentences and 12,458 varying terms of imprisonment. In October 1976, an article written by the GDR Director of Public Prosecutions for the weekly journal "Horizont" indicated that as of that date 12,852 persons had been sentenced in the German Democratic Republic because of their involvement in Nazi crimes.

This figure also includes those sentenced in the "Waldheim trials". The report from the Federal Minister of Justice to the Bundestag President of 26 February 1965 contains the following comments:

> "In that year (1950), the Soviet occupying power wound up its concentration camps on German soil and surrendered 3,432 prisoners to the authorities of the Soviet Zone in order to "have their criminal activities examined and tried by the courts" (letter from General Zhukov to Ulbricht of 14 January 1950).
>
> These prisoners were transferred to Waldheim Penitentiary. Soviet Military Administration Order No. 201 instructed the criminal prosecution bodies of the Soviet Zone to judge the Waldheim prisoners in pursuance of Control Council Law No. 10 and Control Council Directive No. 38. By way of exception, the cases were tried in the "Criminal Division of the District Court of Chemnitz" packed with party-line people's judges and lay assessors. The sentences passed on the Waldheim prisoners between 21 April 1950 and the beginning of July 1950 were without excep-

tion long terms of imprisonment, in many cases penal servitude for life and for 32 of the accused the death sentence. 24 of the death sentences were carried out by hanging during the night of November 1950 in an underground cell.

Together with the Federal Minister for All-German Affairs, the Federal Minister of Justice issued a statement on 5 September 1950, pointing out the numerous infringements of the law committed in the trials and in particular the fact that the procedure adopted by these special courts contravened certain fundamental principles of law which, pursuant to the law of civilized nations, form part of the indispensable legal guarantees inherent in a fair trial. In other words, the Waldheim sentences represented arbitrary justice.

E. The Prosecution of Nazi Crimes in Austria

In 1977, the Austrian Ministry of Justice published a booklet called "National Jurisdiction and the Prosecution of Nazi Crimes in Austria (1945—1972)". It contains statistics showing for the period in question that 13,607 persons were convicted on charges of having committed Nazi crimes and that the convictions included 43 death sentences and 23 terms of life imprisonment. Some of those sentenced came from the "old Reich", i.e. the Reich territory within the frontiers of 1937.

F. Possibilities and Constraints in the Prosecuting of Nazi Crimes

As the report[1] from the Federal Ministry of Justice to the Bundestag President of 26 February 1965 revealed for the first time in regard to the period from the end of the War to the beginning of 1965, the public prosecutors and courts of the Federal Republic of Germany instituted legal proceedings against 67,716 persons suspected of complicity in Nazi and war crimes with a resulting delivery of 6,115 non-appealable sentences.

The apparent disproportion between the two figures attracted sharp criticism of the prosecuting methods practised by the German judicial authorities — particularly when the ratio grew worse during the following years[2]. These figures are still quoted today, mostly by foreign publications, to corroborate the allegation that tens of thousands of recognized and unpunished "Nazi murderers" remain at large in the Federal Republic of Germany without the legal authorities doing anything about bringing them to trial. The baselessness of these charges becomes evident to anyone who makes an effort to take an impartial look at the factors determining the success or failure of the prosecution of Nazi crimes.

I The Identification of Suspects still liable to Prosecution

As the above-mentioned report from the Federal Minister pointed out — although the critics chose to ignore this point — the number of accused is so much higher than the total of those actually sentenced because the authorities initiated a large number of preliminary judicial inquiries in order to be able to examine the records of large administrative departments and even entire police companies or battalions on a man-by-man basis.

When the systematic investigation and prosecution of Nazi crimes commenced in 1959, the inquiries first of all centered on such series of crimes as featured in the available documents and books on this subject. The focus of attention became the crimes committed in the extermination camps, the large ghettos and the forced-labour camps as well as the activities of the operational groups and units of the Security Police and Security Service, various police battalions and SS units. It was known that a large number of persons had belonged to the agencies and units in question during the various periods when the crimes took place. However, only some of these men had been involved in criminal acts in an indictable manner and no-one knew who these individuals were. Nor was it known whether they were still living or whether they had died during the War or in subsequent years. On the basis of staff establishment lists or compilations of identity discs and medal recipients and moreover the results of the first questioning of witnesses or defendants, it nevertheless soon proved possible to establish the names of a large number of former members of the relevant agencies and units. Yet this all remained purely prima facie evidence until the actual offenders and their accessories had been traced.

When the time for the limitation of the crime of manslaughter drew nearer in 1960 and that of murder some five years later (8 May 1965), the public prosecutors became very anxious to interrupt the period of limitation for all suspects, irrespective of whether their subsequent fate was known or not. To this end, formal charges had to be preferred. The rapid rise in the number of accused persons in the years after 1959 — for which the critics now blame the prosecuting authorities — thus resulted primarily from the efforts being made to keep the number of potential beneficiaries from limitation as small as possible.

In a country like the Federal Republic of Germany lacking any central registration system, it proves very difficult to find out the whereabouts of accused persons of whom usually only the name and rank or duties at the time of the crime are known — at least to begin with.

As the investigations have shown and still reveal even today, many of the wanted men either did not survive the War or have died in the meantime. In other cases, their traces disappear somewhere abroad, notably in Arab and South American states where many of them evidently fled[3]. In those countries without any direct interest in bringing Nazi criminals to trial, the German prosecuting authorities cannot undertake any inquiries to establish the whereabouts of wanted persons since INTERPOL does not take part, pursuant to its statutes, in the prosecuting of political crimes — and it regards Nazi crimes as falling under this heading.

As has meanwhile been demonstrated in many cases, the supreme administrative agencies of both the SS and the police furnished their staff with forged identification papers shortly before the end of the War. For this reason, it must be assumed that many of these people who went into hiding after the War remained in the Federal Republic and — if they are still alive — have in some cases not yet been identified[4]. In addition, quite a large number of gravely incriminated suspects traced in the Federal Republic during the investigations were able to point out that American, British or French prosecuting authorities had already examined the crimes of which they were accused and that the legal proceedings had been completed with the passing of sentence or the dismissing of the case. In these circumstances, the provisions of the "Transition Agreement" ruled out a fresh trial by German courts[5].

Sometimes, the judicial inquiries revealed that the accused had been sentenced to death by a foreign court and then executed.

In a few cases, the accused committed suicide shortly after being confronted with the charges[6]. In other instances, the suicide of the accused or defendant took place during detention pending trial[7] or during the court hearing[8]. On numerous occasions, accused persons or defendants died from illness in the course of the legal proceedings — sometimes after the delivery of the judgment but sometimes before the sentence became legally binding[9].

All the numerous cases in which even strenuous efforts did not bring to light the whereabouts of the accused or where the person in question had died before or during the trial — together with those cases in which a rehearing was precluded by virtue of the Transition Agreement — appear in the above-mentioned statistics of terminated proceedings as dropped prosecutions or dismissed charges.

In many cases, the incapacity of the accused and defendants to stand trial as determined by a court-approved medical practitioner ruled out fresh proceedings at a later date or brought about the suspension of an on-going trial. For the same reason, the quashing of a lower-court judgment by the Federal Supreme Court meant in some proceedings that the case could not be retried before a jury-court. It is quite wrong to assume that the courts accepted these medical certificates without verifying them. In numerous instances, the courts ordered the defence to produce further medical evidence or insisted on renewed medical examination by a court-approved doctor. Nor did they hesitate to continue the hearings (in some cases for weeks on end) at the accused's bedside. But in the face of unanimous medical testimony confirming inability to stand trial for medical reasons, a court has no other choice but to suspend proceedings or — if the doctors deem an improvement in their patient's condition to be improbable — to dismiss the case altogether.

The fact that such quashing of proceedings against Nazi criminals due to illness occurs more frequently than in other criminal trials does not lie in the indulgence exercised by the courts — as critics of the German legal system allege — but in the fact that the accused are considerably older at the time of the main hearing than in "conventional" crimes of violence. The following table shows the average age of persons appearing before jury-courts during the last eighteen years on charges of having committed Nazi crimes. The figures refer to their age by the time of the main hearing.

Year	Age				
1961	52.7	1967	59.4	1973	62.6
1962	54.3	1968	58.6	1974	64.4
1963	54.8	1969	61.0	1975	63.8
1964	55.6	1970	61.1	1976	67.2
1965	55.9	1971	61.7	1977	64.8
1966	59.0	1972	62.5	1978	66.0

Anyone studying this table should bear in mind that it refers to accused persons whose state of health did not prevent the holding of a main hearing. An inclusion of those accused persons and defendants unable to stand trial for health reasons would raise the average ages considerably. Whereas the number of defendants in Nazi trials before jury-courts is continuously falling[10], their average age is rising at a rate which no longer corresponds to the time interval since the crime. This fact indicates that more and more of those persons who were older at the time of the crime (30—40 years of age) can no longer be prosecuted. Clearly, this category of persons is likely to contain a larger percentage of the more senior officers or officials.

II The Plea of "Superior Orders"

It would be difficult to name any legal proceedings against Nazi crimes which did not feature this problem. Since the days of the trials before the International Military Tribunal in Nuremberg, defendants have argued time and again that they only committed the alleged crimes in the face of an otherwise inevitable threat to their own life and limb. The Central Office has looked into every case known to it through preliminary or criminal proceedings in which it was firmly alleged that refusal to carry out a criminal order would have resulted in injury to their life and limb. In no single instance was the allegation substantiated. The counsel for the defence of the accused proved unable to present the courts with a single case in which refusal to carry out a criminal order would have entailed an objective danger for the life and limb of the recipient of the order as defined in the relevant legal provisions [11]. Until the Penal Code was amended in 1975, the relevant provisions read as follows:

Art. 52

(1) A criminal office shall not be deemed to exist where the offender was compelled to carry out the deed by irresistible force or by a threat connected with an immediate, non-avertible threat to his life and limb or that of a member of his family.

Art. 54

A criminal offence shall not be deemed to exist where the act was committed, apart from a case of self defence, in an unpreventable emergency arising through no fault of one's own to rescue the offender or a member of his family from an immediate threat to life and limb [12].

The Federal Supreme Court soon had an opportunity in the course of numerous rulings to look into the whole problem of persons acting under binding orders. The following fundamental principles were enunciated as having the most bearing on whether or not the accused can plead superior orders. The recipient of the order must be in **im-**

mediate danger, i.e. a situation which in normal circumstances and pursuant to a further development of the given circumstances makes the onset of injury inevitable or at least highly probable. The mere **possibility** of injury does not accord with the concept of a threat and does not suffice to warrant a plea of superior orders[13]. Hence, the threat of transfer to a probationary or punitive military unit cannot necessarily be recognized as constituting a danger to life and limb[14]. The offender must have used his best endeavours to avert the imminent threat in some way other than by carrying out the criminal order[15]. Moreover, he must have undergone an inner conflict which left him no choice other than to act in the way he did[16]. Such a conflict situation only exists where the offender was expected to do something which he did not really wish to do or which he approved of. Furthermore, the offender must have been conscious of a concrete and imminent threat to life and limb; any threat of which he was unaware cannot have influenced his will[17]. This awareness alone must have been the decisive reason for his actions[18].

An acceptance of the plea of superior orders is excluded where the recipient acted out of sadism, hoped to derive a special advantage, wished to gratify his commander or did not want his superiors to think him incapable[19]. By the same token, an offender cannot claim to have acted under binding orders in a situation where, after his initial attempts to get the criminal orders retracted had failed, he perpetrated a deed in a spirit of resignation and blind obedience because this seemed to him in the given circumstances to be the most convenient way out and the path of least resistance[20]. The requirement is not that the threatened recipient of orders should have displayed heroism; on the other hand, weakness of character and will-power are no excuse[21].

The inability to adduce any single case to show that refusal to carry out criminal orders resulted in injury to life

81

and limb does not appear so astonishing when one bears in mind the fact that non-compliance with an order entailing a special degree of severity was not regarded pursuant to SS ideology (as enunciated by Himmler personally) as disloyalty but as personal weakness. It merely barred the person concerned from further promotion within the SS [22].

One cannot, however, exclude the possibility that there may have existed a situation where a person acted under binding orders in a manner relevant for criminal law at some place and time or other. Be that as it may, there can be no doubt that superior orders do not objectively play such a role as would today permit one to invoke them.

Much greater practical significance attaches to "putative superior orders". As the results of judicial investigations have shown, there is no denying the conviction held by many subordinates or deliberately induced in them by their former superiors that refusal to carry out even manifestly criminal orders would place their life and limb in jeopardy. Such a emergency situation sincerely believed to exist on the strength of false assumptions counts, pursuant to the court rulings, as excluding guilt and frees the person concerned from prosecution. But a court can only pronounce a case of putative superior orders to have existed if the offender can adduce significant reasons to demonstrate convincingly his erroneous assumption that an emergency situation existed and, by the same token, if the general circumstances of the situation indicate that the offender was only induced by this erroneously assumed emergency to carry out the criminal order and not by any other motives.

The difficult and often virtually unsolvable problem confronting the public prosecutors and courts is how to decide which of the accused can invoke the guilt-excluding argument of putative superior orders. This explains why only a few members of a unit or agency involved in a crime actually appear before the jury-courts as accused persons. These are the ones whose agreement with, and zeal in the commission of the criminal act refutes their argument and their belief that they had been faced with an unavoidable emergency situation.

III Acting on Orders pursuant to Article 47 of the Military Penal Code

An important role in the defence put forward by the accused in Nazi trials is the frequent invoking of Article 47 of the Military Penal Code of 10 October 1940. This provision applied not only to the armed forces, but also to members of SS and police units[23].

The provision reads as follows:

1) Where the execution of an order in respect of official duties infringes a penal law, the sole responsibility for this shall be borne by the superior officer issuing the order. His subordinate carrying out the order shall however be deemed to be an accessory
    (1) if he exceeded the bounds of the order issued; or
    (2) if he was aware that the order issued by his superior concerned an act designed to bring about a general or military offence or crime.
2) Where subordinates are guilty to a small degree only, punishment may be waived[23a].

An order in respect of official duties shall only be deemed to exist if it commands a subordinate to carry out a clearly defined act without providing him with any opportunity to use his own discretion[24].

The recipient of an order in respect of official duties can only be punished for the deed he committed in compliance with an order if it is established that he did not clearly discern the criminal intent behind the order given to him[25]. The important consideration is not his legally qualified knowledge: it suffices if his mentality and range of perception made him aware in accordance with his own customary way of looking at things that the ordered act represented something wrong[26].

Where a subordinate has aided and abetted the commission of a murder in accordance with an order in respect of official duties, he may only be spared punishment pursuant to Article 47, para 2 of the Military Penal Code if he found himself in a conflict situation similar to an emergency as a result of the order and where any punishment is bound to appear unjust and intolerably harsh because of the burden resting upon him through the said order.

Only in a few cases have jury-courts trying Nazi crimes availed themselves of the possibility to refrain from inflicting a punishment under Article 47, para 2 of the Military Penal Code.

IV Proof of Guilt

A great deal of surprise has been voiced about the strict requirements laid down by West German courts in Nazi trials as the regards the furnishing of proof. Yet these are the same standards as those stipulated in any other criminal trial conducted along constitutional lines in order to produce enough evidence to convict someone. There is no room in criminal legislation for the concept at the heart of the denazification proceedings that mere membership of an agency or unit participating in a crime provides prima facie evidence of culpable conduct. Even though the accused in Nazi trials refused their victims all legal guarantees and civic rights, our legal system enjoins us to give them these guarantees despite the risk of one or two of them evading justice in this way. Any other approach would be a quest for revenge and thus the basis of fresh injustice.

In some of the earlier Nazi trials, the jury-courts were able to base their verdicts on the most convincing proof possible in a criminal case, i.e. a confession by the accused; today, this plays virtually no role at all. Over a period of years, the accused and defendants in the various criminal proceedings have maintained contact with each other and enjoyed the opportunity of exchanging notes on the experience gained in their trials. Whereas one gained the impression in former years that many defendants became actuated by a need to make a clean sweep of things and confess, the investigating officials and judges of today come up against a wall of silence or subterfuge. The keen awareness of the growing difficulties of adducing evidence and the moral backing furnished by old or new Nazi groups have transformed a former occasional willingness to confess into an inclination to play for time.

Another form of evidence usually lacking in Nazi trials — unlike other legal proceedings against crimes of violence — is the local taking of evidence by a judge visiting the scene of the crime. True, jury-courts from the Federal Republic of Germany have been given an opportunity to carry out such local inspections and gain important findings with which to effect a sound assessment of the memories of witnesses and defendants alike[27]. This has been notably the case in Poland and on some occasions in the Soviet Union. In the overwhelming bulk of cases, however, a local inspection can no longer help to ascertain the true facts because of changes in property and vegetation.

Jury-courts are thus compelled to base their verdicts almost entirely on the testimony of witnesses and on documentary proof. The importance assigned either to the former or the latter in a Nazi trial depends largely on the category of offender to which the accused person or defendant belongs.

As a rule, Nazi criminals may be divided into two major groups. The first group comprises those who issued or passed on the orders — now usually referred to as the "armchair culprits". The second group comprising the actual perpetrators of the crimes and their accomplices may be described as the "physically involved culprits":

the members of the firing squads, the guards and personnel at the concentration and extermination camps, the
drivers of the gas vans — in brief, all those who actually
looked into the eyes of their victims. In some cases, the
dividing line between the two categories may be flexible;
yet when applied to a specific crime, such a distinction is
almost always feasible. The furnishing of proof differs
for the two groups. The armchair culprit, making his decisions on life or death for hundreds or thousands of people far away from the actual scene of the crime, remained
unknown in name and appearance to the victims or non-
involved witnesses and often even to the subordinate offenders. The only witnesses whose evidence may be taken
into account in such a case are usually those people who
worked close to the "mastermind" in question and knew
of the relevant responsibilities and chains of command.
Such persons mostly display great reluctance to come forward because they fear possible implication among the
accused or the possibility of being justly or unjustly incriminated by defendants against whom they given evidence. On this account, the only reliable way to convict
armchair culprits consists in producing documents with
explicit references to his person and role in the crime. By
contrast, the "physically involved culprits", who were
hardly ever individually named on documents relating to
the crime because of their mostly subordinate duties and
low rank, can as a rule only be convicted on the strength
of witnesses' testimony.

The renewed efforts undertaken since 1965 by the public
prosecutors and the Central Office in Ludwigsburg in line
with the Bundestag's instructions to procure all documentary evidence of Nazi crimes obtainable at home and
abroad have brought about a steady increase in the volume of documents at hand for the prosecuting authorities.
As of January 1979, the Central Office housed some
520,000 pages of copied documents whose originals had
mostly been discovered during the evaluation of foreign

archives[28]. These documents are registered under about 2,000 keywords in a subject-catalogue comprising 129,000 filing cards (separately classified in accordance with contents, issuer and recipient of the document and the other named agencies)[29]. It also names the whereabouts of the original documents. In order to make these documents rapidly accessible for the prosecuting authorities and courts, the Central Office drew up 51 lists of documents (mostly with an index of names and places) for internal use: 43 of these lists comprising 300 copies each were then distributed to all agencies in the Federal Republic engaged in the prosecution of Nazi crimes whilst others were only forwarded for use during certain proceedings. To meet the demand which then arose, the Central Office prepared 450,000 pages of photocopied documents between 1965 and 1977 and forwarded them to the agencies concerned.

The copies of documents deposited in foreign archives mostly come from the USA, the Soviet Union, France and Czechoslovakia and other collections from the Netherlands, Belgium, Norway, Israel and (on a smaller scale) from other European countries. The principal contingent — about 80,000 copies[30] — was provided by the Main Polish Commission for the Investigation of Nazi Crimes[31].

The protracted endeavours made to obtain access to the stocks of documents housed in the archives of the GDR such as the personal files of former members of the administrative police and to use them for prosecuting Nazi crimes in the Federal Republic have all been frustrated by the attitude adopted by the competent East German authorities[32]. In the 1960s, representatives of the GDR Director of Public Prosecutions occasionally visited our public prosecutors to hand over certain documents; in each case, these aimed specifically at prominent public figures in the Federal Republic. On the other hand, numerous enquiries made by the Central Office about events at concentration camps located on the territory of the GDR were not answered by the authorities there[33].

The suspicion voiced at the beginning that the documentary records from Eastern states might perhaps be forgeries has now largely died away since it was revealed that those most likely to profit, i.e. the accused themselves, do not avail themselves of this eminently handy argument but instead acknowledge almost without exception the correctness of the documents when confronted with them.

The work of analyzing those items of documents in German archives needed for investigating and prosecuting Nazi crimes had largely been completed by the end of the 1960s. This evaluation had moreover to confine itself to the relatively voluminous categories of documents where the experienced archivists could expect to find relevant evidence. The huge quantities of deposited records made any other approach to systematic analysis appear quite hopeless. At a later stage, however, the archivists took the initiative and provided information for the prosecuting authorities in many cases where they discovered previously unknown material of relevance for investigating Nazi crimes.

Many of these documents are, however, only of use as illustrative background material. As for the other documents, they merely serve — with very few exceptions — as links in a chain of evidence needed to demonstrate objectively and subjectively the crimes with which the offenders are charged. There is a virtually complete absence of written or photographic evidence offering an adequately precise reproduction of the details of a crime, irrespective of other proof, and also permitting a reliable identification of the responsible person and an assessment of his mental attitude to the deed. This in turn implies the impossibility in practice of convicting defendants in a Nazi trial solely on the basis of documentary evidence. Despite the rising volume of available documentary proof, there will still be a need in future for the testimony of witnesses even though that remains the most doubtful form of evidence in terms of objective reliability.

There is no such person as an absolutely objective witness who observes a certain event while in full possession of his senses, stores it in his memory and then proves able after a long passage of time to reproduce the details without making a mistake. One of the court's most difficult tasks still consists in judging the objective veracity of a witness's testimony. Compared with other criminal trials, the obstacles encountered in Nazi cases are much greater because of the almost complete absence of "neutral" witnesses.

Most of the series of murders were carried out under conditions of great secrecy and with the virtual exclusion of third parties. Only in the case of the mass shootings in the East, the "resettlement" of Jews in extermination camps or the "local resettlements" [35] did it prove impossible to prevent some of the local population from hearing about the atrocities. However, their knowledge mostly related solely to the general substance of the occurrences and not to the details on a scale sufficient to permit a reliable identification of those responsible.

Apart from a few exceptional circumstances, the bulk of the witnesses appearing in court during Nazi trials stood, directly or indirectly, by the side of the perpetrators of the crimes when they took place. They were thus linked with them in the widest sense of the term in the performance of joint tasks: often enough, however, the only thing they had in common was the wearing of the same uniform. Some of the witnesses may quite rightly fear implication in criminal proceedings in the event of delivering a truthful statement. They try to avoiding having to tell the truth by indulging in vague observations. Other witnesses perhaps hold back in their statements because they are now ashamed of having known of these events at the time and of remaining silent about them. In some cases, one must allow that they have repressed their memory of former occurrences and now believe themselves to be unable to recall anything. Needless to say, many of the particulars have slipped their minds due to the expiry of so much time. Yet the degree of ostensible forgetfulness pleaded by many witnesses in the court room often strikes listeners as shocking and shameful. The Nazi trials have shown time and time again that those persons (apart from the defendants themselves) who could supply the most effective contribution towards establishing the true facts tend in effect to be the biggest obstacle in accomplishing this.

An equally critical eye must be cast at the statements made by witnesses from among the ranks of the victims who stood close to the offenders. At the time of the massacres forming the subject of a trial, the survivors almost invariably found themselves in a state of extreme emotional and physical stress, i.e. a condition in which, as we know from past experience, their senses failed to register anything not directly connected with survival itself as material. Their memories simply did not record the events. Furthermore, even when they were not in immediate danger of losing their lives, the prisoners in concentration and labour camps experienced continuous emotional strain and thus suffered an impairment of their physical and psychological powers of receptivity. A former concentration-camp inmate, who listened to the proceedings at the Auschwitz trial in Frankfurt and was then due to testify as a witness in a Nazi trial, wrote the following in a letter to the public prosecutor in Cologne:

"Those of us who say we were there at the time are expected to have seen and heard everything. Yet in effect we were nearly paralyzed with fear and terror and our senses almost failed to register anything. We are called upon to name the hour and the day, but we had no clock or calendar in the camp: often, we did not even know if it was a Sunday or a public holiday. We are called upon to describe our executioners, but for us they all looked alike in their uniforms. And then if we make a mistake about one point even though at least 20 years have passed since the offence, our testimony is cast aside altogether."

On numerous occasions, psychologists and psychiatrists were enlisted in Nazi trials to pronounce an expert opinion on the credibility and reliability of memory of such persons as had been subjected to extreme strain a long time ago. They unanimously agreed that impressive events occurring in younger years are easily remembered by older witnesses and, as far as the main happening is concerned, can be reproduced in reliable form [36].

Since the trials of accused persons denying the charge are often decided by subsidiary matters — not discernible for the individual witness — the court's persistent questioning about apparently unimportant details strikes both the witness under questioning and many of the listeners as unnecessary. Admittedly, the counsel for the defence often harasses witnesses with undue severity and sometimes in a highly unfair manner in order to establish the overall untrustworthiness of the witness on the grounds of certain discrepancies, usually of no significance for the trial, which ensue from a comparison with former statements. Now and then, those attending a trial have seen how some witnesses regard requests from the court to be more precise as an attack on their credibility and react with appropriate vehemence. Similarly, witnesses are often taken aback by a calm and objective warning not to digress, but to adhere to the subject of the trial.

It also frequently happens that witnesses from among the victims qualify their former statements made in the preliminary proceedings during the main hearing and offer only hearsay evidence rather than eye-witness accounts.

On some occasions, the apparent inconsistencies between the statements made by a witness during preliminary proceedings and those advanced in the main hearing stem from the fact that he gave his testimony for the preliminary proceedings in a language of which either he or the examining official only had a poor command. This kind of misunderstanding arose, for example, when a statement made in Yiddish was entered in the records in German. It also emerged that witnesses who had frequently met former fellow-sufferers in the years since the War (for example on certain anniversaries) and exchanged memories now find it difficult to distinguish between what they experienced themselves and what they merely heard. It is particularly difficult in these cases because the external framework of their own experiences was congruent with that of what they merely heard. On one occasion, a court ascertained that several witnesses who had read the same memorial book of a Jewish congregation quoted in good faith a certain unimportant detail incorrectly (though objectively) described by the author in the belief that they were reproducing it from their own memories.

The number of instances where witnesses from among the ranks of the victims clearly and deliberately made a false statement is extremely small. According to the observations made by the judges and public prosecutors concerned with the trials, the same applied as a rule to German and foreign witnesses. This fact was noted by the jury-court in Ulm in the opinion it expressed about the statements furnished by witnesses for the prosecution:

> "Broadly speaking, we did not find that witnesses indiscriminately, uncritically and in clearly exaggerated fashion incriminated the accused and consciously or unconsciously availed themselves of the judicial inquiries to blame the defendants for what happened. On the contrary, the witnesses observed in regard to many of the events quoted that they knew nothing of them or at most only from hearsay. They gave one the impression of making a conscious and critical effort to describe their recollections as well as possible ...[37]".

92

Even though a court may have no reason to question the veracity of a witness's statement, it nevertheless holds no guarantee that the witness can correctly and objectively remember what he experienced and reproduce it accordingly. If there is no opportunity for measuring a witness's memory and veracity by means of other evidence such as documents, photographs, a local inspection of the scene of the crime or the testimony of other apparently credible witnesses, the courts evince an understandable reluctance in view of the numerous conceivable sources of error to base a sentence of imprisonment for life or for a term of several years on the statement of a single witness — however trustworthy he may appear. Yet today, there is very often only a single witness for a certain crime.

The number of witnesses available for the Nazi trials is decreasing from day to day. To the losses from death and illness must be added more and more the reluctance and exhaustion of witnesses from among the victims, especially where — apart from Israel — they come from non-European countries or European states which were not occupied by the Germans during the War. No doubt, the frequently vigorous questioning of witnesses by individual defence counsels often reported in the past (particularly in foreign newspapers) discourages many people from appearing before a court in the Federal Republic of Germany. Other witnesses who were imprisoned at the time for reasons other than political or racial grounds entertain fears that they may have to make a statement in a public court hearing, possibly in the presence of friends or relatives, about the reason for their commitment to a concentration camp.

But there is another factor, too. The thousands of German consular officials entrusted with the interrogation of witnesses abroad have commented on the substantial efforts needed to induce witnesses to appear on the stipulated day for the taking of evidence. It emerged in New York, for example, where a large percentage of the Jewish witnesses live that only 50% of those asked to appear were willing to come along for the hearing. Although some make no comment on the reason for not appearing, many explain their unwillingness to make a statement against the background of their fears that a confrontation with the details of former horrible events, which often cost the lives of members of their families, would open up old but healed wounds. Others seem, like many of the accused, to have thrust any recollection of the events from their memories.

One highly dedicated investigating judge, who had questioned a considerable number of witnesses in Australia in 1974 and ascertained to his surprise how little they could remember, made the following points in a report to his Land Minister of Justice[38].

"After questioning more than 20 persons of all age groups, I asked myself why there was a contrast between their statements and those of former prisoners now living in Germany, Poland and Israel, who can clearly remember all the important details of certain events. As many of the Australian witnesses stressed, much may be explained from the fact that they emigrated after their liberation to a country which, unlike all European states, did not have any relationship with the Third Reich however historic this may meanwhile have become. The witnesses had to establish a means of livelihood for themselves amid completely unfamiliar surroundings; they began a new life in every sense of the word and consciously or unconsciously repressed everything that preceded it."

The investigating judge continues his report in a spirit of resignation:

"The real value of the journey for me consisted in my gaining a complete awareness of the dubious nature of investigations at the present point of time, particularly in regard to witnesses living abroad. If I had not personally attended the questioning sessions ... I would have been forced to explain the insubstantial minutes of these meetings with their mostly insignificant contributions in terms of the consuls' lack of experience in Nazi investigation."

By way of summary, we can safely state on the basis of the above-described situation that the fairly rapid decrease in the value of witnesses' evidence in Nazi trials cannot as a rule be made up by the increase in available documentary evidence.

V Procedural Problems in Nazi Trials

The customarily lengthy nature of Nazi trials in comparison with other criminal proceedings has sometimes attracted criticism of the judicial authorities in the Federal Republic of Germany on the grounds of a deliberate or tolerated delay in the administering of justice. But anyone who has taken the trouble to investigate the background and reason for the admittedly very long duration of Nazi trials will soon establish just how unjustified this kind of reproach is. None the less, there is no denying the errors occasionally made and the inevitable delays in concluding the preliminary inquiries and then holding the main hearing.

In the majority of cases, the Central Office had to begin by conducting its initial inquiries "against a person or persons unknown". Once some months or in individual cases even years of investigations had led to the discovery of the whereabouts of one or several persons suspected of having perpetrated criminal acts within the framework of a major series of crimes (such as those carried out by an operational unit or in an extermination camp), the responsibility for initiating formal preliminary proceedings was passed to the public prosecutor competent for legal actions in the district where the principal offender resided. The public prosecutor then came up against the problem of either swiftly preferring charges against the meanwhile identified offender because of his probably demonstrable incrimination in single crimes or else attempting to clear up a whole series of crimes involving a large number of as yet unknown culprits. In practice, this means: should the public prosecutor in Düsseldorf confine himself to the misdeeds of a Kurt Franz or should he initiate the "Treblinka trials"? Should the public prosecutor in Darmstadt investigate the crimes imputed to former SS officer Callsen or examine the "special 4a unit" complex? Ought the public prosecutor in Hamburg to take action against SS Obersturmführer Maywald or extend his inquiries to cover the whole agency run by the Head of Security Police in Riga? Should the central department of public prosecution in Cologne satisfy itself with ascertaining the crimes committed by camp overseer Hackmann or try to open up the whole nexus of events at Camp Maidanek?

Each of these decisions could prove to be right or wrong, although the correctness or error of the decision often only emerged when it became too late. What proved to be correct for dealing with the case of Treblinka Extermination Camp (institution of preliminary proceedings by the public prosecutor in December 1959, main hearing as from October 1964 and delivery of judgment in the first instance in September 1965) need not necessarily apply to Camp Maidenek (institution of preliminary proceedings in February 1962, commencement of main hearing in November 1975 and expected delivery of judgment at the earliest by the middle of 1979).

On numerous occasions, even experienced jury-court judges tried to simplify things by recommending the subdividing of a large series of crimes into several separate proceedings. In most instances, however, such a subdivision was bound to mean in view of the strict rules on jurisdiction set out in the Code of Criminal Procedure that various courts had to examine a complex of crimes that was essentially uniform and coherent: the witnesses (often advanced in years) had to furnish their testimony on the same subject at various times before different courts and frequently travel long distances to do so.

That seems unwarrantable — for more reasons than simply the need to economize on legal expense. Quite apart from witnesses' potential exhaustion at having to give so much evidence, the ascertainment of the whole truth might be rendered difficult by the defendants' attempt in the various trials to play off one against the other. A precise determination of the relatively higher or subordinate rank of the accused, the assignment of duties within a military command and the organization of a unit or camp will mostly only be possible if those concerned appear before a court in a homogeneous trial.

Furthermore, the restricting of the subject-matter of a trial to only a few items detached from a major nexus of cases produces disadvantages as well as benefits. True, it may shorten the period of time needed for preparing and holding the trial: on the other hand, it also risks curtailing the ascertainment of the real historic facts. Needless to say, the business of criminal proceedings consists in establishing the individual guilt of an accused person and not in pursuing research studies on past events. Yet it is difficult to imagine any criminal act other than a Nazi crime where there is such a need to shed light on the overall circumstances and particulars in order to verify the defendant's objective and subject contribution to the deed in question.

Whilst even the ascertainment of the facts establishing the preferred charges takes a comparatively long time due to the difficulty of adducing proof, an equally protracted period of time is required to check the defensive allegations advanced by or even expected from the accused so as to be able to parry these arguments during the preliminary proceedings. Since the burden of proof rests on the public prosecutor, any shortcomings in this field make themselves felt during the trial itself to the advantage of the accused. Once that the offender has been acquitted because of inadequate investigations, any evidence unearthed at a late date serves no useful purpose.

In nearly all proceedings, the defendant pleads superior orders in respect of the crime. The veracity of such a claim can as a rule only be adequately assessed by illustrating the defendant's conduct over longer than just a limited period of time: nothing less than his general behaviour over a fairly extensive period of time will indicate his real attitude to the crime.

Clearly, the perhaps varying knowledge and personal dedication of the investigating officials play a certain role in the duration of the public prosecutor's initial inquiries. But much greater significance attaches in this context to the decision taken by each public prosecutor on his own responsibility as to when the available evidence is deemed adequate for preferring charges and securing the conviction of the suspects. Many an acquittal results from the court's view that the evidence collected by that point of time does not suffice to convict the offender. Many a judgment has been quashed during the appeal stage because the Federal Supreme Court held the view that the jury-court had not exhausted all the available sources of information.

The length of time needed in the various proceedings to obtain evidence often depends on circumstances upon which the public prosecutor exercises only a small degree of influence. When it is a question of tracing and questioning witnesses living abroad or obtaining documents from foreign archives, all that the public prosecutor can do in this field is to politely request the foreign authorities in question to give the matter expeditious treatment. If the defendant names witnesses in order to parry incriminating evidence, the public prosecutor — mindful of this obligation under the Code of Criminal Procedure to ascertain facts likely to exonerate the accused — must follow up these references.

Up to the end of 1974, any preferment of charges in Nazi trials was preceded by preliminary judicial inquiries in the wake of the public prosecutor's investigations. The essential factor determining the length of these judicial inquiries was the approach adopted by the examining judge to his assigned task. On many occasions (particularly in South Germany), the examining judges confined themselves to simply interrogating the most important witnesses as indicated by the inquiries made up to that point in time, i.e. apart from the accused himself. In other proceedings, many judges deemed it essential to hear even the last available witness wherever he might be in the world. These judicial inquiries frequently succeeded in expanding the available results of previous investigations and thus in strengthening their value as evidence. Broadly speaking, however, it can safely be said that the abolition of preliminary judicial inquiries by virtue of the First Law to reform Criminal Procedure of 9 November 1974[39] helped to shorten the duration of proceedings without essentially impairing the substance of the trials proper.

Apart from the duration of preliminary proceedings, there has been a steady increase in the length of the main hearings over the years[40]. The impression often prevailed that the accused's strategy consisted primarily in gaining time and achieving recognition of his incapacity for trial due to illness and only secondly in substantiating his denial of the charges. The fact that courts occasionally accede to a demand from the defence counsel that certain seemingly irrelevant evidence be admitted in case this provides the grounds for the lodging of an appeal becomes all the more comprehensible when one knows of the difficulties arising for the holding of a fresh trial due to an increasing lack of evidence if the court of appeal decides to quash the judgment. The apparently excessive indulgence on the part of a jury-court faced with a spate of applications from the defence counsel for admission of evidence with the resulting protraction of a trial by weeks or months may in fact often have thwarted the reversal of a decision by the appeal court.

Only a knowledge and appreciation of all these circumstances permits one to criticize fairly the manner in which a public prosecutor or court handles legal procedure in a Nazi trial.

The amount of time needed for Nazi trials has increased steadily in the course of recent years. According to the records of the Central Office, the average duration of proceedings (initial inquiries by the Central Office, investigations by the public prosecutor, preliminary judicial inquiries and the preparation for, and holding of the trial itself) amounted to the following number of years up to the pronouncement of judgment in courts of the first instance.

Year	No. of Years	Year	No. of Years
1962	3.6		
1963	4.5	1971	8.2
1964	4.8	1972	8.3
1965	5.4	1973	9.4
1966	6.1	1974	9.1
1967	6.1	1975	11.7
1968	7.4	1976	9.4
1969	7.4	1977	16.8
1970	7.6	1978	12.5

It should be borne in mind when appraising these figures that the investigations made in connection with proceedings commencing during the early 1960s did not make rapid progress because important documents stored in foreign archives were not yet available. A systematic and promising scrutiny could only take place when the public prosecutors finally obtained large quantities of the requisite documentary evidence, i.e. between 1967 and 1970. Even though the knowledge of the historic background which we need to clear up and prosecute Nazi crimes has meanwhile grown with a concomitant sophistication in investigating techniques, these trials will in future still last for several years on an average because of the increasing difficulty of obtaining evidence — i.e. assuming that trials are at all possible in view of the mounting shortage of defendants and witnesses. Preliminary proceedings initiated in 1979 will probably not result in a main hearing (even if all favourable circumstances for the conduct of the case are present) before 1983 or 1984. Moreover, the chance of adducing proof will have deteriorated by then.

The possibility of convicting the accused some 40 years after the crime will hinge more than hitherto on the fortuitous circumstance of whether or not important witnesses are still alive and able to recollect the events.

G. The Current Situation in the Investigation and Prosecution of Nazi Crimes

The important factor in the varying development and current situation in clearing up individual series of crimes is not only the type of criminal involved (armchair culprit or actual perpetrator) and the type of victim (Jew, political opponent), but above all the scene of the crime. The following account has been written with this in mind.

I Crimes 'committed Abroad (excluding Concentration Camp Crimes and those against Prisoners of War)

1. Poland

The current stage now reached in the investigation of Nazi crimes committed against Jewish people in Poland may be described as fairly encouraging, as these deeds were usually carried out by members of stationed units and organizations and moreover as largely systematic preliminary proceedings have been instituted in this field since 1959. In view of the fact that the measures taken against the Jews rested on supra-regional orders, at least one legal action was brought for each rural or urban district set up by the German administrative authorities in the former Generalgouvernement of Poland as well as for each extermination camp, large-sized ghetto and labour camp respectively in order to shed light upon the crimes committed in that area or camp and to detect all the possible suspects.

About 20% of the preliminary and criminal cases tried since 1958 and 30% of the jury-court judgments relate to the killing of Jews on Polish territory[1]. Despite the highly systematic nature of the preliminary proceedings, it will not however be possible to bring to trial all the murderers of Jews in Poland because of the scale and variety of this series of crimes.

The killing of non-Jewish Poles made it difficult to find a promising starting-point for methodical investigation. Legal action could only be taken as and when specific information was furnished about criminal acts liable to prosecution. To begin with, this information came in considerable quantities from the questionnaires which, shortly after the War, were given to each Polish municipal mayor to complete following an initiative taken by the Main Polish Commission. The mayors had to quote as precisely as possible the place and time of the crime, the circumstances of its commission, the discernible cause of the deed, the personal particulars of the victim and a description of the culprits. In the year 1960 (and particularly in 1963 and 1965), the Central Office received several hundred copies of these completed questionnaires and commenced appropriate judicial inquiries. Only in a few cases, however, did the resulting trials lead to the passing of sentences. Quite apart from the fact that the statements in the questionnaires were not always reliable[2], they largely referred to the circumstances surrounding the partial extermination of the Polish intelligentsia during the first months of the War from September to December 1939[3]. To the extent that the persons participating in the crimes were not senior commanders or particularly malicious mass murderers, their contribution to the misdeeds was normally deemed by the public prosecutors' offices and courts — in keeping with the rulings of the Federal Supreme Court — to constitute "aiding and abetting murder". Such crimes as had been committed prior to the coming into force of the Ordinance of 5 December 1939 already became statute-barred on 8 May 1960[4].

On the strength of documentary evidence furnished by the Main Polish Commission during the last few years (comprising the minutes of questionings, sketches and photographs of the scene of the crime) hundreds of cases involving the killing of Polish civilians became known. Since they mostly concerned individual deeds and the culprits (in the few cases where they could be described at all) were usually only known by their surnames — often spelled phonetically — it is quite fortuitous today if living participants can be identified[5]. True, it may seem theoretically possible in some cases — irrespective of whether the crimes were committed in Poland, the Soviet Union or elsewhere — if there is no starting point for identifying the perpetrators, to slowly work through the ranks of possible culprits in the course of laborious investigations which on past experience often last for years. The only way to do this, however, would be to try and find out which military units and organizations were stationed at the scene of the crime or nearby at the time when it was committed so as to ascertain the names and addresses of the members of such units. A questioning of those members still alive might in favourable circumstances produce more precise details of the crime and the possible group of perpetrators. As we know from previous efforts, however, the probability — apart from fortuitous circumstances — of tracing the living perpetrators of such crimes and of adducing sufficient evidence to prefer charges remains infinitely small.

Individual crimes, notably arbitrary acts on a small scale, which may have been committed by unknown members of military units or organizations appear to be no longer normally amenable to a solution even where no doubt exists as to the perpetrator's membership of a certain unit or organization. The solving of these crimes is frustrated by the unwillingness of other members of the unit or organization to furnish evidence and by the unreliable nature of witnesses' testimony due to the passage of time.

104

Sometimes, the records forwarded by the Main Polish Commission merely contain evidence that is so vague and self-contradictory as to indicate beyond doubt the hopelessness of any further inquiries[6]. In some cases, the German prosecuting authorities were unable to prefer charges against the felons or to get them sentenced, because the principal accused persons known by name are dead and the other participants either untraceable or else unconvictable on the strength of the available evidence[7].

Where the combating of Polish resistance movements exceeded the limits of permissible reprisals or punishment under international law and custom of war, it is difficult to establish the characteristics constituting murder (brutality, malice, thirst for blood, baseness of motives[8]); in such cases, the killings are deemed to be manslaughter and hence statute-barred since 8 May 1960.

Because of all these circumstances, there have been comparatively few convictions for the killing (outside of concentration camps) of non-Jewish Poles.

2. The Soviet Union

The first series of thorough investigations to be carried out into the crimes committed by the Wehrmacht in occupied territories of the Soviet Union concerned the activities of operational units and groups of the Security Police and Security Service and the stationed administrative agencies later set up there. The starting-point for these inquiries were the "progress reports for the USSR" described above[9]. As a rule, preliminary proceedings were only opened if and when the testimony of witnesses or accused persons given during other trials definitely revealed suspicious facts. In the meantime, those offenders who could still be apprehended have been brought to trial and sentenced in a large number of jury-court trials.

By contrast, the examination with a view to prosecution of the unchecked activities of the stationed agencies of

105

Security Police and civil administration set up in the areas behind the frontline did not yield any material findings. True, there were numerous references to homicidal crimes. Mostly, however, it proved impossible to determine either the personal data or the current whereabouts of those responsible. The records of evidence (minutes of the questioning of witnesses and the reports of local investigating commissions) submitted by the Soviet Union in Russian usually contained a phonetic spelling of the suspects' names or else such a garbled version as to render identification impossible. Even when the identity of the perpetrators of crimes was occasionally established, it emerged that many of those concerned were no longer living.

The majority of crimes committed in the USSR and capable of clarification involved the extermination of the Jewish section of the population. The killing of non-Jews was usually directly connected with the war against the partisans. There has not, however, been any systematic investigation of these events, which are classified as war crimes[10]. When such incidents become known, the public prosecutors open preliminary proceedings; according to information available to the Central Office, however, only one case has so far resulted in a conviction.

3. Czechoslovakia

Unlike the investigating of Nazi crimes committed in other countries, the main attention in the scrutiny of these crimes in Czechoslovakia did not focus upon the "final solution of the Jewish question". Almost without exception, the Jews from Bohemia and Moravia were sent to the camp at Theresienstadt — long deemed to be a model establishment which foreign delegations could be shown around on a number of occasions. Hence, the impossibility of proving subjectively that those taking part in the deporting of Jews to Theresienstadt were involved in the criminal killings. Hitherto, no one has been able to find out whether, and if so to what extent, the Central Department for Jewish Emigration in Prague played a role in the transfer of prisoners from Theresienstadt to Auschwitz which was later ordered by the Reich Security Office (Dept. IV B4 — Eichmann).

The investigations undertaken to clear up Nazi crimes committed in Czechoslovakia were mostly confined to the incidents in the Gestapo prison at "Kleine Festung Theresienstadt", the pseudo court-martials held in Prague and Brünn, the activities of operational group "H" of the Security Police in Slovakia after the uprising in 1944 and the police brutality unleashed throughout Bohemia and Moravia in reply to the assassination of Heydrich in 1942[11]. Some of the preliminary proceedings undertaken by the public prosecutors' offices have not yet been brought to a close. So far, no charges have been preferred. According to information given to the Central Office, the principal perpetrators of these crimes are now dead. As regards the other participants, the available evidence does not suffice in the view of the public prosecutors in charge of the investigations, either subjectively or objectively, to convict them of having taken part in the murders.

In the course of the last few years, the "Czechoslovakian State Commission for the Investigation of Nazi War Crimes" has on numerous occasions sent to the prosecuting authorities of the Federal Republic of Germany documentary evidence — some of it very comprehensive — on the slaying of Czech civilians. A great deal of it concerned events which took place just before the end of the War during the uprising of the Czech people against the German occupation forces. The investigations have still not been completed in some of the proceedings. In most cases, the evidence produced gives rise to doubts as to whether the circumstances of the killings would constitute murder (which alone is not yet statute-barred).

4. Yugoslavia and Albania

The volume of documentary evidence available on Nazi crimes in Yugoslavia is still very small. The investigations have been confined to Serbia and, regarding the events of Autumn 1943, to Albania [12] since the authorities in the state of Croatia set up in 1941 carried out their measures against political opponents and Jews while acting independently and on their own responsibility.

Apart from the murder of Serbian Jews in the camp at Semlin [13], the proceedings initiated by the public prosecutors in the Federal Republic of Germany have mostly related to individual incidents for which fortuitous evidence turned up. These cases frequently involved offences committed by ethnic Germans against their Serbian fellow citizens and tolerated by the German occupation authorities.

The bulk of the ascertained killings took place as a concomitant of the combating of resistance and partisan organizations by the police or the German armed services. This category of crime also embraces the reprisals and sanctions carried out as a reaction to the attacks against the German occupation forces, often resulting in hundreds of deaths. The investigations effected by the public prosecutors — and the Central Office did not participate as the cases concerned war crimes — suffered from the above-mentioned lack of evidence. Moreover, the documents which the State Institute for Contemporary History in Belgrade has been making available since 1969 have not been able to remedy this deficiency.

5. Greece

As far back as 1954/55, the Greek authorities started to send the Federal Ministry of Justice a series of records referring to crimes committed by German nationals in Greece during the War. However, the preliminary proceedings instituted by the public prosecutors did not lead to the tracing or convicting of the culprits.

In the course of the year 1965, Greece used diplomatic channels to send the German authorities a series of voluminous data on criminal acts perpetrated by German nationals. This material chiefly referred to the same events as had been covered by the cases set in train by the material surrendered in 1954/55. The 200 ensuing preliminary proceedings finally had to be discontinued on the grounds of the death or disappearance of the accused. As nearly all the incidents directly involved the combating of Greek resistance groups and moreover it was not as a rule possible to establish the essential elements constituting murder, the proceedings also had to be terminated because limitation had commenced.

6. Hungary, Rumania and Bulgaria

The legal actions brought by the prosecuting authorities of the Federal Republic of Germany against those guilty of Nazi crimes in Hungary, Rumania and Bulgaria pertained to the wrongs committed during the "final solution of the Jewish question". Over and above the latter, no legal basis existed for the initiation of further proceedings. The three states in question did not respond to the Federal Government's appeal of 20 November 1964 to make available any documentary evidence in their possession for evaluation purposes. However, a number of former members of the German Foreign Office and Reich Security Office have been sentenced for their role in the deporting of Bulgarian and Hungarian Jews to the extermination camps.

7. Belgium, the Netherlands, Luxembourg, Denmark, Norway and Italy

A systematic investigation of the crimes committed by a potential category of persons in Western countries occupied during the War by German armed forces also had to rest solely on the measures carried out under the "final solution of the Jewish question". These preliminary proceedings have now almost been completed. But here again, the public prosecutors have had to terminate most of them because of the death of those suspected of the crimes or because no conduct eligible for prosecution in criminal law could be proved against them. Some hearings did, however, yield convictions. For example, the Commander of the Security Police and the Security Service in the Netherlands, his "Adviser for Jewish Affairs" and another member of his department received sentences on the grounds of having taken part in the deportation of Dutch Jews to the extermination camps. Charges were also preferred against the deputy-Commander of the Security Police. The counsel for the defence lodged an appeal with the Federal Constitutional Court to test the constitutionality of the trial. As of 1 May 1979, no ruling had yet been given.

A large number of preliminary proceedings were also initiated to punish the killing of non-Jews in these countries. These cases were helped by the clues in documentary evidence provided by Belgium, the Netherlands, Luxembourg, Norway and Italy. The bulk of this material referred to events concerning the resistance organizations. As the essential elements constituting murder could not as a rule be proved, the majority of the cases — where the suspects had in fact actually been traced — came to an end after 8 May 1960 due to the commencement of limitation. Only a fairly small number of trials led to the convicting of the accused.

8. France

Similar to other countries, the only point of departure for the opening of a thorough judicial investigation of Nazi crimes in France lay in the wrongs committed there during the "final solution of the Jewish question" in pursuance of the standard regulations and commands issued by the Supreme Reich authorities — the Reich Security Office — for the whole of the German orbit of power existing at that time. The obstacle continually encountered was the limits imposed by the "Transition Law" [14]. Those suspects who could be traced entered the plea that they had already either been sentenced by French military tribunals in France on the same charge or else acquitted. By the same token, it was known in numerous cases that Germans had been sentenced to death in absentia by the French military tribunals. In all these cases, the German prosecuting authorities and courts were prevented from taking any action against the accused.

The public prosecutors pursued their inquiries to the limit of what was legally permissible. An opportunity for examining those Nazi crimes in France which could still be investigated and prosecuted did not present itself until 9 April 1975 when the "Agreement on German Jurisdiction for the Prosecution of certain Crimes" concluded between France and the Federal Republic of Germany came into force and the French authorities thereupon permitted an evaluation of the records at their military tribunals. (See also the observations made in chapter C. V.).

II Nazi Crimes committed in Germany (excluding Concentration Camp Crimes and those against Prisoners of War)

Since German courts were able to punish Nazi crimes perpetrated against Germans within a short time of the end of the War, the ratio of successful investigation and conviction is a fairly high one. The criminal acts executed in Germany outside of the concentration and labour camps mostly produced a large number of witnesses and the names of the perpetrators were mostly known; moreover, the courts could, if necessary, inspect the scene of the crime.

On this account, the convictions secured by German courts during the period from 1945 to 1949 nearly all concerned crimes which occurred in Germany. The proceedings were usually launched after the aggrieved parties or their families lodged a complaint with the authorities against the authors of the crime either known to them personally or fortuitously discovered. There was no official all-embracing investigation of Nazi crimes committed in Germany until 1965 when the competence of the Central Office was extended to cover the researching of Nazi crimes committed within Germany[15]. By that point in time, the crime of manslaughter had already become statute-barred. In addition to the occurrences in the concentration camps, the investigations set on foot after 1965 primarily related to the deportation of Jews from Germany to the extermination camps or the murder of labour-camp inmates and foreign workers.

The inquiry into the role played by members of Gestapo agencies in the deporting of Jews to the extermination camps was carried out along systematic lines. With one exception, however, the proceedings initiated by the Central Office or transferred by the latter to the public prosecutors' offices have meanwhile been discontinued on subjective grounds. In view of the well-documented efforts made by leading organizations to keep the details of Jewish extermination secret even within the ranks of the SS and the police, the plea entered by the accused that they had known nothing of the existence of extermination camps in the "Generalgouvernement" could not normally be refuted with adequate conviction.

Frequently, the proceedings for crimes committed against the inmates of labour camps or against foreign workers derived from information furnished by the Main Polish Commission, but the investigations did not corroborate the alleged crimes which the charges referred to. Moreover, many of the executions of foreign slave workers took

112

place because of an infringement of prescribed rules and regulations (e. g. insulting or physically attacking German superiors or employers, indulging in illicit sexual intercourse with German women etc.). As they lacked the qualifying characteristics of murder, they could only be designated as manslaughter and had therefore become statute-barred.

III Crimes in Concentration Camps

The crimes committed in German concentration camps and costing the lives of large numbers of foreign prisoners had been the subject of several lengthy trials before the occupying powers' tribunals directly after the War. German courts also tried SS guards from the concentration camps and sometimes also the "Kapos" (camp police selected from among the prisoners themselves). As a rule, these trials led to the sentencing of those concerned and in fact they often received long terms of imprisonment[16].

In 1965, the Central Office was instructed to conduct a thorough examination of all concentration camps including subsidiary and branch camps in order to ascertain the potential group of culprits and, where such persons were traced, to institute preliminary proceedings if their crimes had hitherto not been prosecuted. These investigations resulted in a number of trials and further convictions.

As an examination of the subsidiary and branch camps revealed, killings had not taken place in all of these agencies. But some of the subsidiary establishments were just as notorious as the main concentration camps as regards the cruelties perpetrated and the number of deaths in percentage terms. Several of the preliminary proceedings now in the hands of public prosecutors' offices have not yet been completed.

113

Other cases involved the killing of prisoners during the "evacuation marches". Some of these hearings have led to convictions whilst others await completion.

In comparison with other series of crimes, the identifying of the perpetrators by witnesses from among the ranks of the sufferers proved easier in the proceedings against concentration-camp crimes since the witnesses had a better personal knowledge of the evil-doers because of the long periods of direct contact. On the other hand, the prisoners usually did not know the SS men ordered to accompany them during the evacuation marches. Hence, it is often not possible in these cases to identify the culprits.

IV Crimes against Prisoners of War

During the research into crimes committed against Soviet prisoners of war, all prison camps including subsidiary and branch establishments were examined to see whether there had been any selecting and killing of "intolerables" (i. e. Jewish and other politically suspicious prisoners of war) pursuant to operational orders 8, 9 and 14 issued by the Head of the Security Police and Security Service. In many cases, there was in fact tangible evidence of such killings.

Generally speaking, it proved impossible to identify the members of Security Police and Security Service detachments responsible for executing the selected prisoners. The Wehrmacht camp commandants and other officers who may also have been in charge of the camp were invariably older persons at the time when the crimes were committed. The majority of them had already died by the beginning of the preliminary proceedings. At the present time, those still alive today are between 80 and 85 years of age. Only a few of the trials have resulted in convictions.

One type of crime not thoroughly investigated was the killing of Soviet prisoners of war in compliance with the "commissar order". As we know since the trials held by the international military tribunal in Nuremberg, many army commanders did not pass on this order to subordinate units whilst other officers in receipt of the order refused to carry it out.

The executions carried out under the "Bullet Decree" and the "Commando Order" could not be prosecuted after 8 May 1960 as the motives and circumstances of these acts constituted manslaughter rather than murder.

V "Euthanasia"

The legal action taken since 1945 by public prosecutors' offices and courts in Germany in respect of the killing of the insane under various "euthanasia" operations have, in many cases, resulted in the sentencing of those responsible. The investigations pursued in this field can now be regarded as completed.

VI The Supreme Reich Authorities

Since the widening of its competence as from 11 December 1964, the Central Office has also been engaged in examining the role played by members of the principal Reich authorities (i.e. with the exception of the Reich Security Office). This examination extended to the personnel of the German Foreign Office, the Reich Ministry of the Interior, the Ministry of Justice, the Reich Ministry for Occupied Territories, the Commissariat for Estonia & the Ukraine, the Reich Chancellery, the Reichtag, the Party Chancellery, the personal staff of the Head of the SS, the Office of Reich Commissar for Strengthening German Nationhood, the SS Office for Racial and Resettlement Questions and other main SS offices (excluding the Reich Security Office).

As it turned out, by far the majority of these wanted persons had already died or received sentences from courts of the three Allied powers because of their former activities. Others had been investigated by the British, American and French prosecuting authorities; however, the proceedings were terminated without any convictions being secured. Under the terms of the "Transition Agreement", these cases were removed from the purview of German prosecuting authorities[17]. Despite the fact that a number of public prosecutors initiated preliminary proceedings against the few remaining members of the above-mentioned agencies and authorities still at large, they managed to attain a conviction in one case only. By virtue of the amendment to Art. 50, para 2 of the Penal Code coming into force on 1 October 1968, the prosecution of certain cases had become statute-barred on 8 May 1960[18] — even assuming the production of proof that the accused had been guilty of criminal behaviour.

Similarly, the large-scale investigations undertaken by the chief state prosecutor at the Supreme Court of Justice in Berlin against members of the Reich Security Office disclosed that the bulk of the accused were no longer amenable to justice for the above-mentioned reasons. In this series of proceedings, too, most of those responsible could no longer be prosecuted since the amending of Art. 50, para 2 of the Penal Code: sentences were however imposed on members of the "Jewish Department", the protective custody department and the department responsible for the design and operation of the gas vans.

H. Summary

I In view of the fact that we have no knowledge of the number of persons sentenced in the Soviet Union, Yugoslavia and Czechoslovakia, there is no means of determining precisely how many German nationals have been brought to trial at home and abroad since the end of World War II for their participation in, or perpetration of Nazi crimes or war crimes. Estimates put the total at about 70,000[1].

II According to statistics drawn up by the Federal Ministry of Justice on the basis of the Land judicial authorities' annual reports, German public prosecutors in the Federal Republic of Germany opened a total of 85,802 proceedings between 8 May 1945 and 31 December 1978 against individually named persons suspected of taking part in, or committing Nazi crimes or war crimes. At the time when these proceedings were opened, it was not known in the overwhelming majority of cases whether the people concerned were still living and, if so, where they could be found.

As shown in the above-mentioned statistics, a total of 6,440 persons had received **non-appealable** sentences by the end of 1978: this figure included 12 death sentences (prior to the coming into force of the Basic Law abolishing the death penalty), 156 terms of life imprisonment and 114 fines. One person was sentenced under the provisions of the Law on Juvenile Courts.

In point of fact, the number of sentences was presumably somewhat higher. The research work carried out by Ulrich-Dieter Oppitz[2] revealed the probable incompleteness of the notifications by the Land judicial authorities of the judgments which were pronounced between 8 May

1945 and 31 December 1964 and which formed the basis of the report submitted by the Federal Minister of Justice to the President of the Bundestag. If we take into account the estimates made by Oppitz after evaluating all available and relevant records, the number of death sentences comes to 14 and not 12 whilst the total of non-appealable life sentences delivered by the courts up to 31 December 1978 rises to 166.

In at least 574 cases, the accused were convicted after 1956, i.e. at a time when only homicide could be prosecuted following the limitation of less serious crimes.

In 76,750 cases, the proceedings did not end with a conviction. The reasons for this are as follows:

— it proved impossible to ascertain the whereabouts of a large part of the suspects;

— thousands of them did not survive the war or wartime captivity, died after the War, received death sentences from Allied courts and were hanged, died during the proceedings or committed suicide;

— several thousands of them had already been convicted or acquitted by the tribunals set up by the Allied occupation authorities and were no longer amenable to prosecution by German courts for the same offence under the terms of the "Transition Agreement";

— many of the wanted persons escaped to South American or Arab countries after the War and either went into hiding there or were not extradited by these countries to the Federal Republic of Germany[3];

— some of those accused could not be tried because they produced official medical certificates testifying to their unfitness for trial on the grounds of old age or infirmity;

— the preliminary proceedings against thousands of defendants had to be terminated due to lack of evidence or proven innocence in those cases where large administrative agencies as well as police and SS units had to be checked man for man; and

— a large number of accused persons had to be acquitted by the courts because of insufficient evidence.

As of 1 January 1979, law-courts and public prosecutors' offices in the Federal Republic were engaged in either preliminary or criminal proceedings against 2,612 persons believed to have taken part in Nazi crimes. These involved cases where the preliminary inquiries were still in progress, formal charges had been preferred, the main hearing was under way or where a judgment already pronounced by the court had not yet become legally binding. This figure has probably not altered much in the meantime. Although a number of trials have been completed since the beginning of 1979, a substantial series of new proceedings were due to be initiated — a total of 67 between 1st January and 1st May 1979 — on the basis of fresh material meanwhile received from other countries and Poland in particular.

In view of the mounting difficulties inherent in the investigation of the crimes concerned, the production of requisite proof and the length of trials (which can only be abbreviated in the most favourable of circumstances), the prospects of convicting the culprits in recently opened proceedings dwindle from year to year.

III The prosecuting authorities of the Federal Republic will probably continue to detect previously unknown Nazi crimes of violence after 1979. At most, however, these will concern criminal acts involving a relatively small number of suspects and victims. Quite apart from the passage of time, the clearing up of such crimes entails many difficulties because these acts were usually only mentioned in a handful of documents, even at the time of the crime, and moreover only witnessed by a small number of persons. It can be virtually ruled out that any more major series of crimes involving a large number of victims will be detected because the Central Office has been looking since 1959 into all incidents of this kind reported in books and witnesses' testimony or by other methods during the 34 years since the end of the War. It is considered improbable that such events have not hitherto been alluded to somewhere or other. Moreover, the question of whether or not any undetected Nazi crimes concern major series of crimes or merely isolated incidents remains of secondary importance for the assessment of their relevance in criminal law.

IV Since 1960, the limitation of prosecution has been interrupted in thousands of cases. This applies above all to the untraced middle and high-ranking Nazi officials who participated in known Nazi crimes and to particularly malicious mass murderers individually named by witnesses or else described closely enough to be identifiable. Such persons can still be prosecuted after 31 December 1979.

A complete listing of all those persons who participated in Nazi crimes for the purpose of interrupting limitation as a precautionary measure was (and still is) impossible because it must be assumed that not all of the persons in question have so far been named or even described adequately enough to permit unerring identification. Furthermore, the possibility cannot be excluded that some of the many defendants, acquitted by a court after preliminary proceedings had failed to produce sufficient evidence — and without any interruption of limitation having occurred — will be gravely incriminated only on the basis of evidence discovered after 31 December 1979 or not made available by a foreign country till then.

Nevertheless, the chances of bringing to trial Nazi criminals detected after 31 December 1979 are extremely remote for the reasons named above: the age of the accused; the growing difficulty of investigating the crimes and adducing proof; and the relatively long duration of the legal procedure.

120

J. Annexes

I Statistics

Group A: Annual classification of **non-appealable** sentences delivered by German courts in the Federal Republic of Germany in Nazi and war crime cases (Number of persons sentenced)[1].

Group B: Annual classification of preliminary proceedings initiated by public prosecutors in Nazi and war-crime cases (Number per year)[2].

	Group A	Group B		Group A	Group B
1945	23	192	1962	36	814
1946	238	1534	1963	28	559
1947	816	3236	1964	21	810
1948	1819	4650	1965	32[3]	1240
1949	1523	3995	1966	32[3]	489
1950	809	2495	1967	13	544
1951	259	1238	1968	35	685
1952	191	467	1969	30	467
1953	123	301	1970	33	512
1954	44	183	1971	39	528
1955	21	239	1972	26	490
1956	23	262	1973	20	399
1957	43	238	1974	8	358
1958	22	442	1975	28	328
1959	15	1018	1976	14	432
1960	23	1078	1977	7	406
1961	38	934	1978	8	284

1 Statistics drawn up by the Federal Ministry of Justice pursant to the annual returns of the Land judicial authorities (vide also the next table).

2 Up to 1964, the same as[1]: after 1965, pursuant to the records of the Central Office of Land judicial authorities.

3 Median figure for the figure of 64 convictions ascertained for the years 1965/66.

Number of persons against whom public prosecutors initiated preliminary proceedings in Nazi-crime cases during the years 1970 to 1978[1].

1970	1,188	1973	1,301	1976	1,113
1971	1,228	1974	1,499	1977	1,736
1972	1,229	1975	2,235	1978	1,399

Non-appealable sentences and Terminated Cases (without Punishment of the Accused or Defendants) in Criminal and Preliminary Proceedings from 1965 to 1978[1].

Year	Life Imprisonment	Term of Imprisonment	Terminated Cases without punishment
1965[2]	4	28	3186
1966[2]	4	28	3186
1967	5	8	4313
1968	8	27	2581
1969	15	15	2726
1970	10	23	2234
1971	13	26	3859
1972	4	22	2257
1973	1	19	1888
1974	6	2	1233
1975	3	25	1692
1976	1	13	1207
1977	3	4	1709
1978	2	6	2487

1 Statistics drawn up by the Federal Ministry of Justice pursuant to the annual returns of the Land judicial authorities.
2 Average of the totals for 1965 and 1966 (8/56/6372).

Results of criminal proceedings in Nazi-crime cases in which the main hearings were held before jury courts for the first time during the period 1958 to 1978. (Some of the sentences are not final).

Year	Total No. of Accused	Life Sentences	Terms of Imprisonment	Concluded without a Verdict (Case dismissed; no punishment pursuant to Art 42/2 of Military Penal Code; or acquittal)
1958	29	2	15	12
1959	23	4	8	11
1960	22	7	9	6
1961	47	3	29	15
1962	50	4	37	9
1963	49	2	32	15
1964	35	2	16	17
1965	84	14	42	28
1966	77	13	41	23
1967	32	7	18	7
1968	118	23	46	49
1969	50	6	13	31
1970	34	8	13	13
1971	28	3	11	14
1972	28	2	17	9
1973	50	8	25	17
1974	20	6	10	4
1975	11	1	5	5
1976	24	2	9	13
1977	5	1	2	2
1978	4	1	2	1

Classification as % of Accused Persons in Nazi Trials first convicted by a Jury Court between 1958 and 1978.

Group A: Low and middle-ranking civil servants, NCOs and privates, low-ranking Nazi Party officials, former members of ethnic German Self-Protection units, concentration camp personnel etc.

Group B: Executive-class civil servants (inspectors or detective superintendents and above), officers (lieutenants or untersturmführer and above), middle-ranking Nazi Party officials (ortsgruppenführer and above) etc.

Group C: Senior civil servants (governmental counsellor), senior officers (major or sturmbannführer and above), senior Nazi Party officials (Kreisleiter and above) etc.

The figure behind the percentage in each group represents the average age of the accused at the time of the main hearing.

	Group A	Group B	Group C
1958	33.3%/48	45.4%/48	21.2%/50
1959	58.3%/49	12.5%/59	29.2%/57
1960	42.8%/54	21.4%/62	37.5%/54
1961	33.3%/51	50.0%/53	16.2%/65
1962	49.0%/53	30.6%/54	20.4%/62
1963	43.7%/54	45.6%/55	10.9%/60
1964	51.4%/56	37.1%/53	11.5%/60
1965	73.6%/54	16.1%/55	10.3%/59
1966	53.6%/58	30.9%/56	15.4%/61
1967	42.8%/57	37.1%/61	20.0%/61
1968	63.4%/58	25.2%/60	11.4%/61
1969	46.8%/58	40.2%/62	12.8%/66
1970	57.6%/60	33.3%/67	9.1%/65
1971	39.1%/62	56.5%/61	4.4%/68
1972	60.7%/61	35.7%/64	3.6%/66
1973	46.9%/61	46.9%/64	6.2%/64
1974	63.1%/64	31.6%/65	5.3%/73
1975	45.4%/61	36.4%/68	18.2%/68
1976	75.0%/66	20.8%/70	4.2%/67
1977	20.0%/53	80.0%/68	—/—
1978	100.0%/66	—/—	—/—

Activities of the Central Office of Land Judicial Authorities from 1.12.58 to 30.6.78.

Group A: Judicial inquiries initiated by the Central Office in Ludwigsburg.

Group B: Processed items of a general nature (general investigations, replies to requests for information apart from judicial inquiries proper).

Group C: Yearly additions of documents (photocopied pages) to the stocks of the Central Office.

(These figures refer to the period between 1 July and 30 June of a given year).

	Group A	Group B	Group C
from 1.12.58 to 30.6.65	732	15789[2]	85000
1965/1966	314	1473[2]	75000
1966/1967	436	3064	50000
1967/1968	224	2354	60000
1968/1969	124	2031	6000
1969/1970	207	1484	20000
1970/1971	155	633	22000
1971/1972	234	1674	22000
1972/1973	291	1182	10000
1973/1974	245[1]	1474	16500
1974/1975	239[1]	1281	16000
1975/1976	251[1]	1540[2]	40000
1976/1977	386[1]	4743[2]	47000
1977/1978	242[1]	3483[2]	46000

[1] Including the following which were initiated pursuant to records sent by the Main Polish Commission; 1973/74: 167, 1974/75: 157, 1975/76: 198, 1976/77: 155, 1977/78: 218. (Some of the items received from Poland since mid-1978 are not yet "judicial inquiries" because the translation work has not been completed).

[2] These figures include the following queries about compensation matters, personnel identification etc: up to 30.6.65: 4,915, 1965/66: 119, 1975/76: 1,438, 1976/77: 4,008, 1977/78: 2,927.

II The Fate of the Concentration Camp Commandants

Auschwitz

Höss, Rudolf. Executed in Auschwitz (1947).

Liebelenschel, Arthur. Executed in Cracow (1948).

Kramer, Josef. Executed in Hamelin (1947).

Schwarz, Heinrich. Executed in Sandweier (1947).

Hartjenstein, Fritz. Sentenced to death. Died in French prison (1954).

Baer, Richard. Died during detention pending trial (1963).

Bergen-Belsen

Haas, Rudolf. Declared dead in 1950. (Time of death: 31.3.45).

Kramer, Josef. (See Auschwitz).

Buchenwald

Koch, Karl Otto. Sentenced to death by SS court and executed in 1945.

Pister, Hermann. Sentenced to death. Died in American prison.

Dachau

Wäckerle, Hilmar. Killed in action in Russia (1941).

Eicke, Theodor. Killed in action in Russia (1943).

Loritz, Hans. Suicide in Neumünster internment camp (1946).

Deubel, Heinrich (born 1890). Died in 1962.

Piorkowsky, Alex. Executed (1948).

Weiss, Martin. Executed (1946).

Weiter, Eduard. Suicide in Itter/Tyrol (1945).

Flossenbürg

Weisehorn, Jakob. Suicide after discovery of embezzlement (1939).

Zill, Egon. Sentenced to life imprisonment in 1955, later reduced to 15 years. Died in 1974.

Koegel, Max. Suicide (1946).

Künstler, Karl. Killed in action near Nuremburg (1945).

Gross-Rosen

Hassebroek, Johannes. Sentenced to life imprisonment by a British military tribunal. Released in 1954.

Rödl, Arthur. Suicide (1945).

Gideon, Wilhelm. Preliminary proceedings terminated by the public prosecutor.

Herzogenbusch

Grünewald, Adam. Killed in action in Hungary (1945).

Hüttig, Hans. Sentenced to life imprisonment by a French military tribunal. Released in 1956.

Chmielewski, Karl. Sentenced by Ansbach jury-court to life imprisonment.

Hinzert

Pister, Hermann. (See under Buchenwald).

Sporrenberg, Paul. Died in 1961.

Zill, Egon. (See under Flossenbürg)

Kauen

Goecke, Wilhelm. Killed in action in Italy (1944).

Cracow-Plaszov

Göth, Amon. Executed in Cracow (1946).

Lublin-Maidanek

Koch, Karl Otto. (See under Buchenwald).

Florstedt, Hermann. Executed at Himmler's command shortly before the end of the War.

Weiss, Martin. (See under Dachau).

Koegel, Max. (See under Flossenbürg).

Mauthausen

Sauer, Albert. Died in Falkensee/GDR (1945).

Ziereis, Franz. Shot by American soldiers while attempting to escape (1945).

Mittelbau-Dora

Förschner, Otto. Executed (1946).
Baer, Richard. (See under Auschwitz).

Natzweiler

Zill, Egon. (See under Flossenbürg).
Hartjenstein, Fritz (See under Auschwitz).
Hüttig, Hans (See under Herzogenbuch).
Schwarz, Heinrich (See under Auschwitz).

Neuengamme

Weiss, Martin (See under Dachau).
Pauly, Max. Executed in 1946.

Niederhagen-Wewelsburg

Haas, Rudolf (See under Bergen-Belsen).

Ravensbrück

Koegel, Max. (See under Flossenbürg).
Suhren, Fritz. Executed in 1950.

Riga-Kaiserwald

Sauer, Albert. (See under Mauthausen).

Sachsenhausen

Baranowski, Hermann. Died in 1939.
Loritz, Hans. (See under Dachau).
Eisfeld, Walter. Died in 1940.
Kaindl, Anton. Sentenced by a Soviet military tribunal to life imprisonment. Died in the Soviet Union.

Stutthof

Pauly, Max. (See under Neuengamme).
Hoppe, Paul Werner. Sentenced in 1955 by a jury-court in Bochum to 9 years' imprisonment. Died in 1974.

Vaivara

Aumeier, Hans. Executed in Poland (1948).

III Fate of the Commanders of Security Police and Security Service operational Groups and Units[1].

Operational Group A

Stahlecker, Franz. Died from his wounds in Russia (1942).
Jost, Heinz. Sentenced to death in Nuremberg, later pardoned and released (1951).

Operational Unit 1a

Sandberger, Martin. Sentenced to death at Nuremberg, later pardoned and released (1953).

Operational Unit 1b

Ehrlinger, Erich. Sentenced in 1961 by a jury-court in Karlsruhe to 12 years' imprisonment. Verdict set aside by the Federal Supreme Court. Proceedings were terminated in 1969 due to the defendant's continuous incapacity to stand trial.

Operational Unit 2

Batz, Rudolf. Suicide while in detention pending trial (1961).
Dr. Strauch, Eduard. Sentenced to death in Nuremberg and immediately extradited to Belgium where he died in prison (1955).
Dr. Lange, Rudolf. Soviet prisoner of war. Further fate unknown.

Operational Unit 3

Jäger, Karl. Suicide while in detention pending trial (1959).

---

1 Where the operational units went into action near the front lines, they were sometimes known as "special units of the Security Police and Security Service".

Operational Group B

Nebe, Arthur. Executed in March 1945 in connection with the events of 20 July 1944.

Naumann, Erich. Sentenced to death in Nuremberg and executed.

Operational Unit 7a

Blume, Walter. Sentenced to death in Nuremberg but later pardoned and released (1953).

Steimle, Eugen Karl. Sentenced to death in Nuremberg but later pardoned and released (1954).

Rapp, Albert. Sentenced to life imprisonment by a jury-court in Essen (1965).

Operational Unit 7b

Rausch, Günter. Died during preliminary proceedings (1964).

Otto, Adolf. Sentenced to death in Nuremberg but later pardoned and released (1958).

Rabe, Karl (born 1905). Proceedings instituted by the public prosecutor in Hamburg not yet completed (as of 1.10.78).

Operational Unit 7c

Prof. Six, Franz. Sentenced to 20 years imprisonment in Nuremberg, but released in 1952.

Klingelhöfer, Waldemar. Sentenced to death in Nuremberg, but later pardoned and released (1956).

Körting, Erich (born 1902). Charges dropped because of permanent incapacity to stand trial.

Operational Unit 8

Dr. Bradfisch, Otto. Sentenced in 1963 by Hanover jury-court (which incorporated a verdict by a Munich jury-court of 1961) to 13 years' imprisonment.

Richter, Heinz. Sentenced by Kiel jury-court to 7 years' imprisonment.

Schindelm, Gerhard. No clarification of his post-War fate obtainable.

Operational Unit 9

Dr. Filbert, Alfred. Sentenced by Berlin jury-court in 1962 to life imprisonment.

Schäfer, Oswald. Acquitted by Berlin jury-court in 1966.

Wiebens, Wilhelm. Sentenced by Berlin jury-court in 1966 to life imprisonment.

Operational Group C

Dr. Rasch, Otto. Indicted in Nuremberg but incapable of standing trial due to illness. Died during proceedings.

Dr. Thomas, Max. Suicide (1945).

Operational Unit 4a

Blobel, Paul. Sentenced to death in Nuremberg and executed.

Dr. Weinmann. Erwin. Declared dead in 1949.

Steimle, Eugen Karl. (See under Op. Unit 7a).

Operational Unit 4b

Hermann, Günther. Sentenced to 7 years' imprisonment by Düsseldorf jury-court in 1973.

Braune, Fritz. Sentenced to 9 years' imprisonment by Düsseldorf jury-court in 1973.

Dr. Haensch, Walter. Sentenced to death in Nuremberg, but later pardoned and released (1955).

Meier, August. Suicide during detention awaiting trial.

Körting, Erich. (See under Op. Unit 7c).

Krause, Waldemar. Proceedings terminated in 1976 due to his incapacity to stand trial.

Operational Unit 5

Schulz, Erwin. Sentenced to 15 years' imprisonment in Nuremberg, but released in 1954

Meier, August. (See Op. Unit 4a).

Operational Unit 6

Dr. Kroeger, Erhard. Sentenced by Tübingen jury-court to imprisonment for 3 years 4 months.

Mohr, Robert. Sentenced by Wuppertal jury-court in 1976 to 8 years' imprisonment.

Biberstein, Ernst. Sentenced in Nuremberg to death, but later pardoned. Released in 1958.

Operational Group D

Ohlendorf, Otto. Sentenced to death in Nuremberg and executed.

Bierkamp, Walter. Suicide (1945).

Operational Unit 10a

Seetzen, Heinz. Died in Hamburg (1945).

Dr. Christmann, Kurt. Proceedings terminated due to his incapacity to stand trial.

Operational Unit 10b

Persterer, Alois. Shot in Austria (1945).

Jedamizik, Eduard. Died during preliminary proceedings (1966).

Operational Unit 11a

Zapp, Paul. Sentenced to life imprisonment by Munich I jury-court in 1970.

Dr. Bast, Gerhard. Victim of a murder with robbery (1947).

Schulz, Paul. Whereabouts unknown. Probably dead.

Operational Unit 11b

Müller, Bruno. Died in 1960.

Dr. Braune, Werner. Sentenced to death in Nuremberg and executed.

Operational Unit 12

Noske, Gustav. Sentenced to life imprisonment in Nuremberg, but released in 1951.

Dr. Müller, Erich. Post-War fate not clarified, but believed to be in Argentina.

IV Notes

Notes on A

1 Reich Law Gazette, part I, p. 83.

2 For a definition and description of protective custody, see Martin Broszat "National-Socialist Concentration Camps 1939—1945" in his work "Anatomie des SS-Staates", volume 2, p 15ff, published by Deutscher Taschenbuch Verlag, Munich 1962.

3 Abbreviation for "Sturmabteilung".

4 In full, the "National-Socialist German Workers' Party".

5 Generally speaking, "Konzentrationslager" (concentration camp) was abbreviated to KL in official usage but to KZ in popular speech.

6 Federal Archives R 43 II/389.

7 The SS, abbreviated from "Schutzstaffel", originated within the SA as a kind of body-guard for Hitler and later developed into a semi-military organization.

8 Another man marked out for murder, the diplomat Baron von Ketteler, was able to escape by invoking the protection of former Reich Chancellor von Papen, who was then sent to Vienna as German ambassador. V. Ketteler was murdered in Vienna a few days after the "Anschluß" between Austria and Germany in March 1938.

9 Reich Law Gazette, part I, p. 141. The "Enabling Law" permitted the Government to enact laws without the participation of Parliament and this procedure was adopted throughout the Third Reich.

10 "Law on Measures of National Self-Defence". Reich Law Gazette, part I, p. 529.

11 See footnote 14.

12 Only these establishments were designated by the SS officially as concentration camps. In addition, there were a number of other wartime prison camps — notably in the occupied territories — which were administered by senior SS and police officers or by the heads of the Security Police and Security Service. These camps were often erroneously designated as concentration camps.

13 Buchenwald, for example, had 120 and Dachau 150 subsidiary and branch camps.

14 The Reich Security Office under the Head of the SS, Heinrich Himmler, consisted of the Secret State Police (Gestapo), the

133

Criminal Police and the Security Service (= SS intelligence service for home and abroud). The SS Economic Administrative Office, a senior executive department of the SS, was responsible for SS economic interests including the use of concentration camp inmates as labour.

15 In Sachsenhausen, prisoners were put to death in mobile gas-chambers during "trial gassings".

16 The expression "Kristallnacht" or "Reichskristallnacht" for the pogrom staged on 9th and 10th November 1938 was coined in Berlin. It is an allusion to the many shattered shop-windows of Jewish stores.

17 The first restriction already occurred on 7 April 1933 with the enactment of the "Law to restore the Status of Civil Servants" (Reich Law Gazette, part I, p. 175) whereby non-Aryan officials were to be retired. A major encroachment on the lives of Jews resulted from the "Nuremberg Laws" (Reich Law Gazette, part I, p. 1, 146) of 15 September 1935. Under the terms of the "Reich Citizens Law", they were deprived of their status as German citizens. The "Law on the Protection of German Blood and German Honour" prohibited, inter alia, marriage and sexual relations "between Jews and Citizens of German or racially kindred extraction".

18 An investigation undertaken after the War revealed that the figures named in the Report by former Gestapo Chief Heydrich are too low.

19 According to a report submitted by Himmler to Hitler at the end of December 1942, the number of Jews killed in the fight against guerillas alone in South Russia, the Ukraine and Bialystok during the months August to November 1942 inclusive amounted to 363,211. This should be compared with the figure of 9,902 partisans killed in action or shot immediately after capture and that of 14,257 "guerilla sympathisers and suspects" who were executed.

20 At the time of going to press (1 Oct. '78), the main hearing of the legal proceedings against the German guards and personnel at Maidanek Concentration Camp is still in progress.

Notes on B

1 It is interesting to note that about the same time a group of German resistance fighters close to the Kreisau Circle laid down the principle that those responsible for crimes should be brought to trial after the War. (See P. Schneider and H. J. Meyer: "Rechtliche und politische Aspekte der NS-Verbrecherprozesse" — a lecture delivered during the studium generale at Mainz University (p. 10) during the Winter term 1966/67.

2 On the use of the generic term "war criminal" during the trials before the international military tribunal in Nuremberg, see chapter C.I.

2a Of the 12 persons sentenced to death, 10 were executed. Göring committed suicide. Of the other accused, Hess is still in Spandau prison whilst von Schirach and Speer were released on 1 October 1966 as was Dönitz, too, after completing his sentence. Von Neurath and Raeder have meanwhile died.

3 The facts quoted in this chapter largely originate from the report submitted by the Federal Minister of Justice to the Bundestag President on 26 February 1965. — Bundestag Document IV/3124.

4 See chapter C.I.

5 See Telford Taylor "Die Nürnberger Prozesse", Europa Verlag, Zürich 1951.

6 Commencing with the pardons granted by the American High Commissioner John J. McCloy of 31 January 1951, punishments were reduced after 1951 (with the exception of death sentences) and the convicted prisoners were all released by 1958.

7 All those serving various terms of imprisonment were also set free in 1957.

8 Bundestag Document IV 3124, p. 10f.

9 "Trybuna Ludu" of 5 July 1978.

10 The figure of 16,819 convicted persons cited in the Federal Minister of Justice's report of 26 February 1965 (Bundestag Document IV/3124) comes from a Polish publication: it includes Polish nationals charged with collaboration with the Germans and punished by Polish courts.

11 The "Kameradenschinder Prozesse" held before German courts during the 1950s revealed details of how German prisoners of war interned in Yugoslavian camps were tortured into confessing that they had committed war crimes by fellow German soldiers working for the Yugoslavs. As a result of these forced confessions, an unknown number of German prisoners of war were sentenced to long periods of imprisonment.

Notes on C

1 Customary expression for the trials of those accused of committing crimes in direct connection with the Nazi régime.
2 Official gazette of the Control Council of 30 November 1945, p 20 et seqq.
3 Official gazette of the Control Council of 20 December 1945, p 50 et seqq.
4 "Prohibition of the retroactive application of a penal statute".
5 By comparison, secondary importance attached to the acts constituting a crime against peace: these were unique until that point in time in that they were unknown both in the German and foreign penal codes. The only one among the accused to be condemned by the International Military Tribunal in Nuremberg solely by applying the then non-codified legal characteristics of a crime against peace was Rudolf Hess.
6 See appendix No. I.
7 Vide Ulrich-Dieter Oppitz "Strafverfahren und Strafvollstreckung bei NS-Gewaltverbrechen", Ulm 1976, p 30.
8 Official gazette of the Allied High Commission, p 54
9 See chapter C.I.
10 Law A-37 of the Allied High Commission of 5 May 1955 (official gazette of the Allied High Commission p. 3,267) annulled Law No. 13 on jurisdiction in the reserved areas and set aside the provision on jurisdiction contained in Control Council Law No. 10, which had become obsolete through changing circumstances. The criminal acts and threats thereof listed in Articles I and II of Control Council No. 10 were not invalidated until the enactment of the "First Law to terminate Occupation Law" of 30 May 1956 (Federal Law Gazette Part I, p. 437).
11 Pursuant to the version of Article 212 of the Penal Code valid at the time of the crime, manslaughter was fundamentally punishable with penal servitude for life or a minimum term of five years imprisonment.
12 In order to distinguish between murder and manslaughter as well as between the commission of a crime and aiding and abetting in its commission, reference will only be made for the sake of clarity to such court rulings as were delivered during the period subsequent to the years dealt with in this section (1951—1955).
13 Prior to the amending of Article 211 of the Penal Code by the statute of 4.9.41, a murderer was deemed to be someone who deliberately killed another person "with premeditation" without there being any need to establish any further, more aggravating circumstances. In the case of a murder committed before 4.9.41 and only coming up now for judgment, the Court must ascertain whether

the essential elements of murder are fulfilled under both the old and the new wording of Article 211.

14 Neue Juristische Wochenschrift, 1953, p. 1440.
15 **Federal Supreme Court. 2 Penal Law 243/64.**
16 Federal Supreme Court in "Criminal Cases" vol. 18, p. 37.
17 Federal Supreme Court 2 Penal Law 455/55.
18 Regular rulings of the Federal Supreme Court.
19 Federal Supreme Court in "Criminal Cases", vol. 3, pp 180 and 246.
20 **Federal Supreme Court, 1 Penal Law, 110/70.**
21 Superior Court of Justice in Berlin (Kammergericht), Appeals in **Criminal Cases 294/65.**
22 Federal Supreme Court in "Criminal Cases", vol. 18, p. 87.
23 The amended version of the Penal Code valid since 1 January 1975 now set outs a full legal conception of the offender — which was lacking in the old legislation. Accordingly, punishment shall be inflicted upon anyone whose acts — irrespective of whether or not committed at the wish of an accomplice or accessory — constitute the full crime. Hence, anyone who has killed a person by his own acts in a brutal or malicious manner, from thirst for blood, base motives or subject to the other conditions named in Article 211 of the Penal Code shall be punished as a murderer and not as an accessory to murder, irrespective of whether he acted in accordance with his wishes as the principal in the first degree or merely wished to promote the criminal act committed by the other person.
24 On the subject of limitation, see chapter C III.
25 Federal Law Gazette Part I, p. 307.
26 Decision by the American High Commissioner of 31.1.51.
27 Of the 14 accused originally sentenced to death by the US Military Tribunal in Nuremberg, six were already free by the end of 1955. A further three were released between 1956 and 1958.
28 Federal Law Gazette Part I. p. 1,378.
29 On the subject of the limitation of Nazi crimes, see chapter C III.
30 Federal Law Gazette part II, p. 405 and the official gazette of the Allied High Commission p. 3,267.
31 Those who did not come under the amnesty were Germans who had been sentenced (usually to 25 years imprisonment with hard labour) by Soviet military tribunals, sometimes because of genuine crimes but also sometimes simply because they had taken part in some military function or other in the attack on the Soviet Union.
32 In 1958, he was sentenced by a jury-court in Ulm for aiding and abetting murder to 12 years penal servitude. The same court imposed sentences of between 3 and 15 years on the nine other persons also accused of participation.

33 The Central Office of the Land Judicial Authorities in Ludwigsburg should not be confused with the central departments set up by the public prosecutors in Dortmund and Cologne, which act as the coordinating bodies in conducting proceedings against Nazi crimes pending in North-Rhine Westphalia. (Until the Summer of 1978, these crimes were subdivided into mass crimes and crimes perpetrated in concentration camps).

34 In 1964 and 1965, this jurisdiction was extended to cover all Nazi crimes. The only exceptions apart from incidents involving the Reich Security Office were the judicial inquiries into the activities of the People's Court. In these two cases, the competent regional bodies were the Berlin courts and prosecuting authorities.

35 The guidelines adopted by the Land Ministers and Senators of Justice in April 1965 in respect of the Administrative Agreement explicitly stated that war crimes did not fall within the competence of the Central Office.

36 According to the Progress Report submitted by the Central Office on 1 July 1978, the Central Card Index — comprising alphabetical, geographical and military-unit indexes — contains 1,200,000 entries. The number of places or areas mentioned was 3,600. Moreover, there were references to 520,000 pages of documents (see the list in appendix J). Within the space of 12 months, the Central Office distributed more than 60,000 pages of documents to official agencies in the Federal Republic of Germany engaged in investigating and prosecuting Nazi crimes. The Central Office's index of legal actions contains entries on over 12,000 preliminary and criminal proceedings classified in accordance with the scene of the crime and the reference number assigned by the public prosecutors or central departments. Apart from a few exceptions, the entries refer to such cases as were initiated by the public prosecutors after the Central Office had commenced its activities at the end of 1958. A total of 19,000 cases dating back to the period 1945 to 1958 are classified under various headings.

37 Federal Supreme Court, 1 Penal Law, 540/62.

38 Bavaria: Law and Ordinance Gazette GV Bl 46, p. 289.
Bremen: GV Bl 47 p. 83.
Hesse: GV Bl 46 p. 136.
Württemberg: Government Gazette 46 p. 171.
South Baden: Official Gazette 46 p. 151.
Rhineland-Palatinate: GV Bl 48, p. 244.
Württemburg-Hohenzollern: Government Gazette 47, p. 67.
British Zone: Ordinance Gazette 47, p. 65.

39 See chapter C 2.

40 Reich Law Gazette part I, p. 2,378.

41 The draft law was justified by its supporters on the grounds that normal criminal prosecutions would not have been possible for German courts directly after the end of the War, but at the earliest from the Autumn of 1949. "Bundestag Drucksache" (Parliamentary Document) II/1738 and Bundestag Protocols III/46 pp 6,679 et seqq.

42 Manslaughter in particularly grave cases (Art. 212, para 2 of the Penal Code) — which, similar to murder, is liable to life imprisonment — also became statute-barred because the determining factor for the period of limitation remained the customary penalty for the offence in question, i.e. a minimum sentence of ten years imprisonment for manslaughter.

43 See in this context Bundestag Protocols IV/170, p 8528, 8539 and IV/175 p 8778, 8783 et seq and 8786. At that time, the Federal Republic did not yet maintain any diplomatic relations with Poland and Czechoslovakia.

44 Members of the Chief State Prosecutor's Office at the Kammergericht in Berlin also had an opportunity to study smaller collections of documents in the GDR's State Archives in Potsdam. According to a upi report, the President of the Supreme Court in the German Democratic Republic announced on 23 November 1964 that the GDR Archives housed huge quantities of material which would incriminate tens or even hundreds of thousands of Germans.

45 A suitable Note was forwarded through diplomatic channels to those states with which the Federal Republic of Germany maintained diplomatic relations.

46 It was later announced that these (undoubtedly genuine) documents had been available at an earlier date. The report about the spectacular find had — it was alleged — only been disseminated in order to unleash a campaign against the imminent limitation of Nazi crimes. (Ladislaw Bittmann "Geheimwaffe D", SO1 publishinghouse, Bern 1973, p. 59 et seqq.

46a Bundestag Document IV/ 3124.

46b Bundestag Document IV/2965 (new).

47 Bundestag Document IV/3161 and IV/3162.

48 Federal Law Gazette part I, p. 315.

49 See appendix J I.

50 See appendix J I.

51 Federal Law Gazette part I, p. 503.

52 Federal Supreme Court, 5 Penal Law, 658/58. The constituent elements of brutality and malice were not affected by this as elements relating to the crime itself.

53 Bundestag Protocols of the 5th Parliament p. 13,055.
54 Resolution 1158 of the United Nations' Economic and Social Council (ECOSOC).
55 Convention on the Non-Applicability of Statutory Limitations to War Crimes and Crimes against Humanity — 2391 (XXIII).
56 Of the 42 other states which did not accede to the Convention of the UN General Assembly, the following countries were among those which based their negative decision on the prohibition of retroactive laws contained in their national legislation: the USA, Great Britain, Sweden, Norway and Turkey.
57 See chapter C IV.
58 The interruption decisions obtained in 1964 and 1969 mean in these cases that the prosecution of such crimes can — at least theoretically — be continued until 1994 and 1999 respectively.
58a Bundestag Document IV/4220.
59 Federal Law Gazette part I, p. 1065f.
60 See appendix J I.
61 See appendix J I.
62 On the question of what constitutes murder, see the observations made in chapter C II.
63 As the Central Office operates along the same lines as a public prosecutor's office without actually being one, it cannot terminate any judicial inquiries it may have instituted by a decision to drop the charges. For this reason, it transfers the case to a public prosecutor declared competent pursuant to Article 13a of the Code of Criminal Procedure if further investigations undoubtedly and obviously appear to be futile.
64 See appendix J. I.
65 The stipulation in Article 27 of the amended Penal Code that an accessory shall receive a less severe punishment than the offender of the first degree does not exercise any influence on limitation (Art. 78, para IV of the Penal Code). In accordance with currently valid law, the aiding and abetting of a Nazi murder committed after 5 December 1939 will, just like the principal crime, not become statute-barred until 31 December 1979. — See Article 309, section V of the Introductory Law to the Penal Code of 2.3.74.
66 Federal Law Gazette part II, p. 431. The first initiative in this direction was taken by the public prosecutor (central dept.) in Cologne.

Notes on F

1 Bundestag Document IV/3124.
2 Compare annex J. I.
3 Examples of those traced in South America are: Adolf Eichmann, Adviser on Jewish Questions at the Reich Security Office, Dr. Bohne, who for a certain length of time was Head of the Euthanasia Organization "T 4"; Franz Stangl, the Commandant of Treblinka Extermination Camp; Gustav Wagner, the seriously incriminated "Terror of Sobibor Extermination Camp"; Walter Rauff, the departmental head at the Reich Security Office responsible for the use of the gas vans; Josef Mengele, the camp doctor at Auschwitz; SS Untersturmführer Eduard Roschmann, representative of the Head of Security Police and the Security Service in Riga.
4 The following may be cited to illustrate the assumption of aliases: the former SS and Police Chief for Galicia Friedrich Katzmann (died 1957), who lived undetected under the name of Bruno Albrecht; the former Commandant of Auschwitz, Richard Baer, who called himself Egon Neumann; the senior SS and Police Chief in Wartheland and later in the Generalgouvernement, Wilhelm Koppe, who lived as Herr Lohmann until his detection in 1960. The Adviser on Jewish Questions in Dept IV of the Security Police in Oslo, Hellmuth Reinhard, declared dead after the War, was traced by a member of the Central Office because he had remarried his "widow" under his former name, Patzschke. Similarly, the former Head of Security Police and Security Service Operational Unit 11 a Paul Zapp, who had been living under the alias Friedrich Böhm, was tracked down in 1976 by a member of the Central Office.
5 See chapter C. II.
6 For example, the former driver of a gas van used by an operational unit stationed near Minsk.
7 For example, Karl Jäger, the SS officer in charge of operational unit No. 3.
8 For example, Kurt Bolender, a member of the camp personnel at Sobibor Extermination Camp.
9 For example the Commandant of Treblinka Extermination Camp, Franz Stangl, who was extradited from Brazil at the request of the Federal German Government for punishment and sentenced by Düsseldorf jury-court to life imprisonment. However, he died in prison before the verdict became final.
10 See annex J. I.
11 By way of contrast, there is also evidence of numerous cases where individuals or even whole units firmly refused to carry out illegal shootings without any of them suffering injury to life and limb. (Examples from Nazi trials with references to sources may be

found in Herbert Jäger: "Verbrechen unter totalitärer Herschafft", Walter Verlag, Olten und Freiburg, 1967).

12 The Penal Code in its amended version of 1 January 1975 contains the provisions on the plea of superior orders in articles 34 and 35.

13 Federal Supreme Court 3 St R 353/54.

14 Federal Supreme Court 1 St R 117/56. There is no need to elaborate the point that a mere demotion after refusing to carry out a criminal order cannot be viewed as an injury to life and limb.

15 Federal Supreme Court 4 St R 500/62.

16 Federal Supreme Court 4 St R 156/61.

17 Federal Supreme Court 2 St R 531/61, 4 St R 500/62.

18 Federal Supreme Court 1 St R 27/50, 1 St R 791/51.

19 Federal Supreme Court 4 St R 156/51, 1 St R 27/50, 1 St R 117/56, 4 St R 359/56.

20 Federal Supreme Court 4 St R 500/62.

21 Federal Supreme Court 3 St R 341/51.

22 See the Posen (Poznan) Speech delivered by Himmler. Documentary evidence 1919 PS at the international military tribunal in Nuremberg.

23 Federal Supreme Court 1 St R 55/55. Even article 3 of the "Ordinance on Special Jurisdiction in Criminal Cases concerning Members of SS and Police Units acting on Special Operations" dated 17.10.39 (Reich Law Gazette part I, p. 2107) decreed that military penal law shall be applied to this category of persons.

23a Control Council Law No. 10 provided for a reduction in punishment in the case of merely obeying orders. (See chapter C I).

24 Federal Supreme Court 2 St R 441/66. The order under which the Security Police operational groups carried out their series of killings is regarded as an order in respect of official duties (Federal Supreme Court St R 121/64).

25 Federal Supreme Court 2 St R 327/67.

26 Federal Supreme Court 4 St R 121/55.

27 As indicated by a report appearing in the Polish newspaper "Trybuna Ludu" on 23 December 1977, the Polish authorities have provided an opportunity on 60 occasions to foreign courts — mostly from the Federal Republic of Germany — to carry out local inspections in Poland and to hold part of the hearing (the questioning of witnesses) there. In addition, judges, public prosecutors and lawyers were enabled in 560 cases to inspect documentary evidence, take part in the questioning of witnesses and view scenes of the crimes.

28 Where members of the public prosecutor's offices were able to obtain documents from foreign archives, they forwarded copies to the Central Office on a regular basis. Copies of those documents stored

in German archives and always freely accessible to the prosecuting authorities are only kept by the Central Office in exceptional cases. When it receives inquiries, the Central Office refers the person concerned to the competent archives and if possible quotes the shelfmark or call number.

29 The Catalogue quotes a large number of documents to be found in the Federal Archives (including the Military Archives), the Bavarian State Archives in Nuremberg and the Institute for Contemporary History in Munich.

30 This figure does not include the minutes of interrogations, photographs or slides and sketches of the scene of the crime sent in the form of complete records.

31 Pursuant to the above-mentioned report in the Polish newspaper "Trybuna Ludu", the Main Polish Commission has hitherto forwarded the German prosecuting authorities 18,400 copies and 130,000 microfilmed pages. But these include a large percentage of duplicates as the Main Polish Commission frequently sent copies of the same document to a number of public prosecutors. Quite often, the duplicates were requested by German public prosecutors engaged in sifting items in Polish archives because they did not know or remember that the copy in question was already available.

32 A number of photocopies of items from the personnel files of the administrative police in the GDR were sent to the Central Office by the Chief State Prosecutor of the Soviet Union.

33 In some of the proceedings pending with the public prosecutors' offices (e.g. the "Sachsenhausen trial"), the GDR authorities have furnished genuine help.

34 In numerous statements on the reasons for their verdicts, the jury-courts have expressed their views in detail on this particular problem.

35 See chapter A. IX.

36 The reader's attention is drawn to an expert opinion furnished by the Director of the Psychiatric and Neurological Clinic at Heidelberg University, Professor von Baeyer in the journal "Der Nervenarzt" 41/70 on pp 83—89.

37 Judgment by Ulm District Court of 8 September '69 — Ks 4/67.

38 Reference No. 30 UR 3/73, Cologne District Court.

39 Federal Law Gazette part I, p 3393 ff.

40 At the first Auschwitz trial opened at Frankfurt jury-court in December 1963, the main hearing of 20 accused persons lasted one year and eight months. In the criminal proceedings instituted against the commander and five other members of the "units of foreign nationals" (Ukrainians, Lithuanians and Latvians) stationed at Trawikni near Lublin, the hearing at Hamburg jury-court

lasted from December 1972 until June 1976. (The "Trawikni units" under German officers were used in Poland during operations for exterminating Jews). The longest hearing of all will probably be the trial of 14 members of the German personnel from Maidanek Concentration Camp. At the time of going to press, the main hearing (which was opened by Düsseldorf jury-court in November 1975) was still in progress. It is thought that the examination of witnesses will last until at least the Summer of 1979.

Notes on G

1 No attempt has been made in the following account to subdivide and compute the proceedings in accordance with the various categories of crime as there was often overlapping within these legal actions and this would thus necessitate detailed explanation. As regards the total number of preliminary and criminal proceedings and jury-court judgments, see appendix J. I.

2 For this reason, the Main Polish Commission later arranged for town mayors to be circularized once again.

3 See Chapt. A. VI et seq.

4 See chapt. C. III.

5 As those taking part in the crimes were often local policemen, it may be assumed that identification would have been possible by consulting the personnel files of the "Main Constabulary Office", presumably kept in GDR archives. See chapter F IV.

6 It is not known whether the Main Polish Commission is also forwarding material which does not contain any references to the whereabouts of non-identified offenders to the prosecuting authorities of the German Democratic Republic or Austria or whether it is assumed there that all non-identified Nazi criminals are necessarily living in the Federal Republic of Germany. On many occasions, the Main Polish Commission transmitted as evidence the minutes of questioning sessions which were 10 years old or even older. In the view of the competent public authorities, their timely transmission could have made a substantial contribution to ascertaining the truth in a number of the trials then in progress but since completed.

7 This applies, for example, to the mass murder committed at the Gestapo Prison of Radogoszcz near Lodz where 900 Polish prisoners were killed by setting fire to the building and machine-gunning all those attempting to escape.

8 See chapter C II.

9 See chapt. A. VII.

10 See chapt. C. III on the jurisdiction of the Central Office.

11 Reference should also be made in this context to the "punishment" of the Czechoslovakian village of Lidice when every single house there was destroyed, all the male inhabitants shot and the females deported to labour camps. Some of the children, whose physical traits rendered them "capable of Germanization", were sent to Germany. No clear answer has yet been given about the fate of the children from Lidice. Several clues indicate that they were killed in gas van at Chelmno extermination camp.

12 The Italian Fascist régime, whose troops had occupied Albania until then, was overthrown in September 1943.

13 In 1955, jury-courts in the Federal Republic of Germany sentenced the former Commander of the Security Police and Security Service and in 1969 one of his men to several years imprisonment for aiding and abetting the murder of Jews in Semlin.

14 See chapt. C. II.

15 See chapt. C. IV.

16 At the time of going to press, the main hearings in four cases involving crimes committed in concentration camps are still in progress.

17 See chapt. C. II.

18 See chapt. C. IV.

Notes on H

1 The starting point for the Report issued by the Federal Minister of Justice on 26 February — Bundestag Document IV/31124 p. 37 — was a larger number on the assumption that the 16,819 sentences referred to in a Polish publication exclusively involved German nationals (see footnote 10 in section B).

2 Oppitz loc. cit., p. 77.

3 An example of this is the man who designed and directed the gas vans used in the killing of Jews, Walter Rauff, a former Gruppenleiter at the Reich Security Office now living in Chile.

145

Rückerl, Adalbert, 1925-
  [Strafverfolgung
nationalsozialistischer Verbrechen
1945 bis 1978. English]
  The investigation of Nazi crimes,
1945-1978 : a documentation / by
Adalbert Rückerl ; translated by Derek
Rutter. -- Hamden, Conn. : Archon
Books, 1980.
  145 p. ; 23 cm.

  Translation of: Die Strafverfolgung
nationalsozialistischer Verbrechen
1945 bis 1978.
  Includes bibliographical references.
  ISBN 0-208-01883-2